Praise for That Th!nk You Do

"Carrabis throws a lot for thought into a short span. I enjoyed every word."

"I smiled at the ways Carrabis gets his points across. Bravo!"

"The chapters are long enough make a point, yet short enough to not wear out the reader. Leaving one chapter, I was enthusiastic about starting the next, and I loved the clever chapter titles."

"Approaching male/female relationships from refreshingly unique directions, Carrabis educates us in such an engaging, comprehensive way that you'll be tempted to write a thank-you note."

"I'll be sending a copy to a relative who's studying to become a counselor."

"Carrabis shares some astute insights into the human condition and differences between the sexes based on solid research and personal observations. He offers these up with a pinch of humor, making reading this book feel like chatting with an old friend."

"If you ever wonder how to entice that pretty thing across a crowded room, how to recognize if someone's attention is genuine, how to let someone know you're both interested and interesting, how to know if someone's toxic by watching how they move, or how to flirt without getting hurt, this book's for you."

"I wish my therapist had the sensitivity and understanding Carrabis has."

That Th!nk You Do Volume 2: Relationships & Romance

Joseph Carrabis

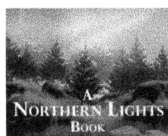

A
NORTHERN LIGHTS
BOOK

ISBN 978-1-969641-00-8

Library of Congress Control Number

Editing by Jennifer Day, Susan Carrabis

Front cover image by John Bernard Scullin

Book design by Jennifer Day

Printed and bound in the United States of America

First printing September 2025

Published by Northern Lights Publishing

www.northernlightspublishing.com

For Susan
(because everything should be)
And AJ
(who said I could)

Special thanks to
Jennifer "JenBitch" Day
who said "We should make a book out of this!"

and

Joseph Della Rosa
who explained LifeHack to me

And of course thanks to all the people through the years who asked me to
talk, chat, help, guide, and teach.
I doubt I did any of those things, really.
I just helped them find their own doors.

And mostly thanks to my Grandpa
who taught me a variation of Mr. Magorium's
"Life is an occasion, rise to it!"

Note to readers:
You can agree or disagree with anything written here and I offer a
suggestion for both:
take a moment to understand and appreciate what causes the
agreement and/or disagreement. Such is the beginning of all
knowledge.

Also by Joseph Carrabis

Contents

Tales Told 'Round Celestial Campfires

Author's Note

These chapters originally appeared between 2008 and 2016 as blog posts on my That Think You Do blog. My work and research covered a number of fields, my work was recognized in many of them, and much of that appeared as these blog posts.

The language used in this book may offend some readers. My goal is to use all the tools at an author's disposal and all the tools in my author's toolbag to create as exacting a sensory experience for the reader and to be as accurate to my creation as possible. Sometimes that means language which may offend some is used to create such exacting sensory images. I've learned to accept my limitations and hope you'll do the same.

Characters, events, places, and things described, depicted, or referred to in this work are fictitious. Any similarity to actual persons, events, places, or things is purely coincidental.

Please be aware this book is not a substitute for professional and medical help. I am not a mental health professional, and nothing in this book is intended to diagnose or treat illness of any kind. If you are currently in distress or crisis, please put this book down immediately and find assistance. Here are some US-based places to start:

- National Suicide Prevention Hotline: 1-800-273-TALK (8255)
- Veteran's Crisis Line: 1-800-273-8255, press 1
- Emergency Medical Services: Call 911
- Substance Abuse and Mental Health Services Referral Helpline for general mental health information and to locate treatment services in your area: 1-877-SAMHSA7 (726-4727)
- FindTreatment.gov
- MentalHealth.gov

Non US-based readers are encouraged to reach out to organizations in their local communities.

Editor's Note

When I first read these pieces I was fascinated to learn more about how humans interact and communicate. Fun facts and life hacks and whoa-that's-interesting. Some stuff I've noticed but never *noticed*.

When I was editing this collection into a book I had new questions. I tried to think like a reader - like you. A lot of the chapters on romance and relationships talk about how men or women behave in different situations, or what interests them. I wondered, "How would someone in a same-sex relationship use this book? How would someone who is not cisgender or who is gender non-conforming use this book?"

Some chapters deal with neurophysiology, some deal with social/cultural factors. I am cisgender female and some of the things about women were very eye opening for me. "Is that so? Huh!"

Joseph and I discussed this, and the answer ends up being pretty simple. No volume of That Th!nk You do is a rule book or instruction manual. It's a way to understand your fellow humans and yourself. Be curious; don't get hung up on specifics.

And that applies regardless of how you identify.

If you want to know more about how Joseph thinks about the

world and how to live, turn to the back of the book and read the appendix on Principles.

Two of my favorites that can apply here:

"If you can't think outside the box then you'll spend your life as someone else's package."

"Own your history. Don't be owned by it."

Enjoy the book!

-Jen

That Th!nk You Do Volume 2: Relationships & Romance

Avoiding Deadly Silences

You know those movies about families' hidden stories? Everybody's happy and smiling and chuckles on the outside and anger and distrust and betrayal are like lava flows waiting to erupt leaving death and destruction in their wake?

Usually the climax is around a meal, a dinner table. Some little comment is said by this person and that person erupts. Or the child says something that only a child could say and the family suddenly has to deal with great uncle Poopah's crimes against humanity.

There are reasons these types of things usually happen during meals. I've mentioned in presentations and trainings that there are two times when humans are biologically most vulnerable: when we're putting stuff into our bodies and when we're pushing stuff out of our bodies. Most people have had the experience of gathering around a table with an extended family and friends. Few people then gather en masse in the loo.

The science of group, tribal and family behavior aside, there's often much that goes unsaid in human relationships. You don't like that they put dishes in the sink rather than the dishwasher. They don't like the way you put toilet paper on the roll (men, did you know this one?).

Seem a little...umm...ridiculous? Small? Meaningless? Irrelevant?

Of course they do and of course they are. Their very triviality is what gives them their power.

Your significant other should know better, right? I mean, who doesn't know there's a preferred direction that toilet paper should come off the roll? Why would anybody leave dishes in the sink when it's just as easy to put them in the dishwasher?

Here's what you may not know about these little irritations that cause such major eruptions — people, feeling their life going out of control, will exert increasing control over trivial annoyances before they make any attempt to deal with major annoyances. They mistakenly believe controlling the small irritations they gain control over the large irritations.

Who Holds Back More, Women or Men?

What's your guess? And let me up the ante while I'm asking. Do the genders go silent for the same or different reasons? Studies done at Fairhaven College and the University of Houston indicate that men resort to silence more often than women do but the reasons are different. Men use silence to maintain power (to keep their partner "on their toes") or because they simply don't know how to express themselves (and women everywhere are nodding in agreement and ask, "You needed a scientific study to know this?").

Women use silence because culturally and historically they have been second class citizens (women are really nodding now). Second class citizens' role is to listen, not to speak, hence their emotions, feelings, wants, needs, and desires go unannounced and unnoticed by their partners.

What is true for both sexes? That self-silencing is dangerous. It causes depression and the more one self-silences the more one becomes depressed. Depression untreated is a death of the soul, folks, so let me share some methods for bringing both your and your partner's souls back to life.

Avoiding the Silences

While there is no guarantee, talking and sharing our wants, needs and desires often cures depression... or at least lets us know the individual we're talking and sharing with isn't as involved in the relationship as we'd like them to be. Talking and sharing — using certain guidelines — allows us to take back control or at least know what we can control in our lives.

And you need to know that talking and sharing — avoiding the silences — is hard work if you've never done it before. I wish I could say it's easy, it's fun, it's as lively and exhilarating as a game of Go Fish with a three-year old and I'd rather have you err on the side of caution than not. Here are some rules to help start the conversation and avoid the silences:

- *Be open and honest.* You want the other person to respond openly and honestly to you? Then be open and honest with them.
- *Listen as much as you talk.* Telling the other person to be quiet and pay attention turns them into a victim and you into the victimizer. Avoiding the Silences is as much about sharing as it is about getting things out, so listen and talk, not just one or the other.
- *Talk about yourself, not them.* An important part to building and healing relationships is sharing your thoughts and feelings, not telling someone what their thoughts and feelings should be.
- Falling from the above, *It's about expression, not approval.* Imagine yourself sharing openly and honestly and hearing "That's not true" or "How can you say that?" or even "I thought so". The latter are statements of approval

and disapproval. You don't want to hear them, neither does your partner. The goal here is to get things out, not notch scores in each other's psyches.

- *Recognize they're not going to be comfortable with this.* After all, are you? The secret is to allow, honor and accept each other's discomfort. Think of this as the big aHA and it'll allow you to see each other as people rather than problems.

- *Accept pushback.* Chances are that until you and your partner are comfortable avoiding the silences there'll be pushback, a desire to not accept responsibility or even some finger-pointing. First thing, pushbacks are defensive, they're not offensive. Want to know the easiest way to respond to a defense? Get inside it. Make allies and not enemies. Ask "How can we solve this?" or "How can we avoid this in the future?" First, "we" are going to work on this together and b) the word "problem" or something similar isn't used.

- *There's responsibility, not blame.* Notice I didn't write "blame" in the above? Blaming people for something may make you feel better and the feeling won't last because blame keeps everybody rooted in the past. Responsibility recognizes the past and plans for the future. Very different. For most people, simply thinking of "blame" then thinking of "responsibility" accesses different neural resources. "Blame" puts someone under a spotlight, "responsibility" puts them on a path.

- From the last two we get *Language is important.* How can I say this? "Sticks and Stones may break your bones but words can mutilate you for life"? "It's not what you say, it's the way you say it"? Everybody knows language can hurt. Most people also know things may slip out when we don't want them to. The good news is you can ask for a "do over". But you do have to ask for the "do over" and you do have to be prepared to hear a "No" in return. In all cases, think before you speak.

- *Touch and only when you both know it's safe.* Human beings need to be touched by others for several reasons and especially when we're in vulnerable situations like this. Touching someone, reaching out to them when we're being vulnerable and when we've accidentally hurt them, is our way of finding out if it's safe. Things may be shared that are painful. How do we heal the hurt? Go back to childhood: kiss the boo-boo to make it go away. But only when our partner is willing, ready and able. They may be unavailable because they need to do their own healing first.

- And that brings us to our last suggestion, *Healing takes time.* Avoiding the Silences work is going to open some wounds, some minor and some not. Wounds take time to heal, and they may not heal as fast as we like. Remember that it will take as much time to get out of the woods as it took to get in, so give both you and your partner time to heal when doing this work. Even better, offer to help each other to heal. Nobody likes being in these kinds of woods alone, especially at night.

Romancing Real Women

... and I don't have to write more because I've already got everybody's attention

Men, pay attention:

Taunus swung the axe effortlessly, almost gracefully for a man his size. Up, over, down and the wood split evenly, almost willingly, cleaving cleanly in two and falling to either side of the stump he used as a brace. He took a neckerchief from his back pocket and wiped the sweat from his brow. Catching Raina staring at him, one hand raised to block the setting sun from blinding her, he smiled and pantomimed his circus-strongman origins at her until they both laughed. Suddenly she screamed. A bear reared over their daughter, Greya.

Greya, sitting in front of the cabin playing with the cornstalk doll Taunus made for her, turned.

The bear waved its forepaws over the child. Greya held her doll up towards the monster as if offering her toy to a friend. Suddenly there was a silent blur and Taunus stood between Greya and the bear. Just stood. Unmoving. Calmly breathing. His dark eyes smiling at the bear. Raina heard his voice, low, soothing.

Greya giggled.

Raina focused but still couldn't hear.

The bear lowered itself to all fours. It sniffed in Taunus' direction, growled something — or said something, Raina couldn't be sure — and trundled off.

Taunus turned and lifted Greya in his arms, tickled her until she laughed, kissed her, lowered her to her feet and nudged her in Raina's direction. The child waddled off towards her mother.

Greya safely beside Raina, Taunus walked back to the wood-pile. The sun glistened off his back, the old wounds receding as they realized today there would be no battle.

Or:

Taunus moved quietly but not so quietly Raina wasn't warned of his approach as he left the surrounding wood. She whispered, "What game today?" She kept her eyes closed and stretched on the blanket, enjoying the tickles of sunlight on her face. Behind her their daughter, Greya, cooed as she played with the cornstalk doll Taunus made for her.

Suddenly Raina felt her face in shadow. Small flowers gently took over the sunlight's tickling role. She looked up to find Taunus kneeling beside her, showering her with petals of rose, oleander, and orange blossom.

His eyes echoed his words, "Every morning I wake and know there's one more day of memories I have of you."

He bent over her and she welcomed his soft, hesitant kiss. She pulled him closer, returning his kiss, letting them linger for a moment in the warmth of the setting sun, the warmth of their many years together.

Greya's doll fell between them and the child giggled. They
pulled away from each other, laughing and smiling.
Suddenly another shadow engulfed them all. A bear, rearing,
waved its paws over them.
Taunus threw what petals remained in his hand at the bear.
"Argos, old friend. Have you lost your honey?"
The bear fell to all fours, sneezed at the sun and trundled off.
Raina pointed after the bear. "Greya, go find some honey for
your pet. Father and I have things to discuss."
Greya picked up her doll and waddled to where the bear
waited, then the two of them went deeper into the
surrounding wood.

Pick one that you think will get a woman's attention.

Take your time. Think about it. Got your answer? Good. The
truth is these two similar fantasy narratives are very demographic
dependent. Specifically, age demographic. The first one will catch the
attention of most women up to about seventy-five years of age and
might even go beyond with some. The second one will catch the
attention of women between 35-55 definitely, then the outliers in
decreasing numbers.

(and yes, I'm talking in general here, not in specifics)

The other interesting aspect of the two is that the former is designed
to attract younger women more so than older women. Mature
women will appreciate the former but the latter fantasy will stay with
them.

I can offer a day long class in the specifics of what each narrative
does and how it works, and let's keep it simple. In romance, in
marketing (just another form of romance in case you didn't know),
in sex (just another form of marketing in case you didn't know):

Appreciate your woman's (or audience's) life and their experience.

The former was written to appeal to people starting out in life, in a world with possible threats and dangers and hardship, a world still in need of heroes and heroines. The latter is designed to appeal to people who recognize not all threats are what they seem, that sometimes laughter is more attractive than heavy-breathing, that years don't make one old, only wiser, and that play can be more seductive than strength.

Let them know you value them for what they offer you.

The former Taunus wouldn't play strong-man unless Raina was there to see, the latter Taunus values each day's memories of her.

Make moves together and you'll rarely move apart.

This one, I admit, assumes the woman in question is a partner and not a conquest. Then again, you probably wouldn't have read this far if your only goal was one of conquest. The former Taunus protects the child without resorting to violence and waits until mother and child are safe. The latter Taunus lets Raina know his interest and lets her decide her interest, then the two decide together.

What most men won't find obvious in either narrative (and women will recognize quickly enough) is that Taunus is comfortable with who he is. He never has to prove anything to himself, to Raina, his child or the bear.

So the secret to being with a Real Woman? Be a real man.

Tripping the Light Fantastic

In my younger days I was quite the dancer. I was invited to both the East Coast Finals and the Montreal Internationals mumbledy-mumbledy years ago and have studied Cape Breton Step Dancing with Step Dancing Masters Bette Matheson and Bonnie Jean MacDonald, among others. Susan (wife, partner, all things wonderful to me) and I still dance when and where we will and I do still love to feel myself move.

Dancing goes way, way back in humankind's psyches, back to the most primitive aspects of our histories. Dancing, more than anything else, is a demonstration of reproductive fitness, what Charles Darwin recognized as "a sexually selected courtship signal". That's Darwin's way of saying nobody goes clubbing wearing sackclothes.

Throughout history dance has served as a physical demonstration of reproductive fitness. More recently dance is used to demonstrate another aspect of reproductive fitness and I'll lay odds that most people don't know what that is.

It's all in how you move...

Both men and women can learn a great deal about themselves and others with a few dance lessons. No need to become a master hoofer, just learn to sense, feel and respond to some simple rhythms, to sense, feel and respond to someone else's motions, sense, feel and respond to another person's wants, needs and desires, learn how to communicate your wants, needs and desires in obvious and nonobvious ways, learn when to move slow and when to move fast, learn when to make big moves and when to make little ones, where and how to hold, when, where and how to lead, when, where and how to be led...

Anybody need a breather yet?

Learn the basics of four steps — Rhumba, Swing, Waltz and Two-Step — and you've learned enough. You'll be able to demonstrate mobility, locomotor skills, bodily symmetry, ..., all those things that make you look nice on the dance floor. That's the physical part.

Those are great and not enough.

...because your moves signal your "confidence"...

Both men and women can benefit from dance lessons because the modern purpose is to demonstrate confidence in your movements and that confidence comes from knowing how to move. I wrote in "Romancing Real Women...and I don't have to write more because I've already got everybody's attention" that one thing women really appreciate in long term relationships is a confident partner.

Learning to dance gives one the opportunity to demonstrate body confidence and a sense of physical and personal space, something women (more than men in western society) also tend to appreciate.

...and confident people (especially males) tend to be non-threatening people.

People who are confident in one thing — even if it's just that they know how to dance — tend to be confident (if not comfortable) in other things. They know how much risk to take and when to say they've had enough. More importantly in relationships, they don't have to prove themselves to anybody and they know how to give other people their own space, mentally and physically.

So want to let someone know you're worth their relationship-time?

Learn how to dance.

I Love the Way You Say That

Ladies, do you enjoy hearing your partner talk? Sing? Hum?

There's something to be said for whether you do or don't. You do: chances are you've found your life long mate. You don't: chances are your relationship won't last much more than...well...than a few matings if that long.

It seems that females are more sensitive to their "family" sounds than males are (generally speaking, of course). The best example of this is the mother who can hear and isolate her child's cry of distress amongst all the sounds of all the activity on a playground.

Well, this auditory sensitivity extends to life-partners and would-be life-partners, too. Women tend to bond more closely with males whose voices are a natural harmonic of their own.

Natural harmonic?

Can you imitate your partner's voice really well? Not just the way they talk or the words they use, but the actual tone of their voice? Can they do the same with yours? Congratulations, your voices are probably natural harmonics of each other. You may not be exactly an octave apart (musically speaking) and chances are you're either close or a multiple of it.

There are lots of reasons this sensitivity leads to long-term relationships: hearing our own "voice" makes us comfortable and puts us at ease, it demonstrates acceptance by the group, things like that. The cognitive and sociologic factors are numerous, really, and seem to play across cultures.

So the next time you're in a meeting and you find yourself mildly interested or a little attracted to someone speaking, listen carefully...you probably are, anyway.

I Want To Hold Your Hand

There's a lot I can write about the psychological and emotional benefits of holding hands, of simple touching, of the bonds it establishes, the communications it ensures.

But that's not the subject today. Today it's about determining if the male in your life will be a good provider in the modern world and one other thing. They're both a simple determinations, really.

Take a moment and look at your significant male's hand. Is his ring finger longer than his index finger? How much longer?

It seems that males whose ring fingers are relatively long when compared to their index fingers are better at risk-taking and have quicker and better responses to challenges in life. For one thing, according to researchers at Northumbria University, it means they're better at making money than most others.

This applies to business partners as well as life-partners. The moral may be to check the hand you shake when next you partner up, inside business or not.

The good news is that I have large hands, sensitive hands, hands that my family told me meant I would be either a pianist or a surgeon. I do play piano and once trained as a butcher's apprentice.

Not quite surgery as most of the patients died. My fingers are long and slender, both ring fingers noticeably longer than my index fingers, and I have a good grip (milking cows all those years, I guess).

The bad news is that this data is, at present, speculative. There's evidence, simply not enough for the findings to be considered worth holding onto, as it were.

The other item I mentioned earlier goes...umm...hand in hand with the previous. It has been proven that males with long ring fingers tend to a variety of psychological challenges. It turns out that the prenatal development of gonads and fingers is linked. Both are controlled by the same genes. The high fetal testosterone that makes little babies into boys controls the length of fingers and creates a predisposition to things like moodiness, melancholy, depression, ...

The benefits of all this? Well, aside from being male, increased musical ability, mathematical and language skills, right-hemisphere brain growth and lower risk of heart attacks.

Oh, great. Long lived, babbling psychotics who can balance checkbooks and sing on key.

I mean, when next you hold your partner's hand, ...

Seeds and Their Trees

Ladies, have you met someone special, someone you think might be the one?

Very good. Excellent. I'm happy for you.

Now a much more important question. Have you met his family? Did you spend time with them? More than an afternoon, more like a weekend. Did you get a chance to see them in the morning, at the dinner table, in the evening, making lunch, going to worship, working in the yard, ... ?

And if you did, what did you think?

It turns out that the adult interactions between males and their families of origin are excellent indicators of their hidden side, their angry side, their possibly violent side.

I want to make clear that I'm not making light of this. It's one of those things that brings tears to my eyes. The hidden scars of childhood physical, sexual, and emotional abuse are often completely undetectable in western males once they're in their 30s and 40s. The scars have to be hidden. There'd be no way for western males to function in society at any level without developing some incredible coping mechanisms.

But what are the signs in the family?

Talk

Listen to the conversations around a meal and when everyone is chipping in to do some chores. Are the conversations one directional, more from parent to child or from one sibling to another? When the child or other sibling speaks up, is it actually speaking up — more defensive or counter-attack — than conversation? Be on guard.

But does everyone get a chance to have their say? Do others listen attentively, even if they make a joke after something is said? And are the jokes about the ideas, not the person presenting them? Is there discussion in which challenges to the norm are accepted and perhaps even encouraged? Very important, if someone says a topic is making them uncomfortable do the others take their conversation elsewhere or force their views to be heard? When people are respected you know that you will be respected.

Play

Does the family or members thereof play games? Does only one person win, all the time? And if someone else wins, is there a silent tension taking place?

Or are the youngest siblings allowed to win? Is open, obvious cheating followed by riotous laughter or anger and disgust? Do people play to win or vanquish?

When anyone can and does win, goodness follows.

Chores

Do family members help according to their ability or do one or two people take everything on while others watch? Is there a team functionality or superstars? Is one person given a "bye" for no obvious reason? Do people willingly put their own interests off to take part?

And if they do, do the other family members work harder or faster so the one sacrificing won't have to sacrifice too much?

Males and Their Aggressive Genes

It turns out that some males lack a gene that produces monoamine oxidase (MAOA). MAOA is important because it keeps different parts of the brain in touch with each other. While any child abused in childhood — male or female — will be dealing with issues as an adult, males lacking MAOA who suffered childhood abuse were four times more prone to violence as adults.

How do you know if your chosen male is missing some MAOA? Well, you don't. Not without a biolab, anyway. But what you can do is see them in relation to their family. It turns out that this is a real case of nature versus nurture. Males missing some MAOA who were raised in affirming, loving families had no out of the ordinary challenges as adults.

And what if you can't see them around their family? Then ask them for their stories. Is there a lot of love in their childhood memories? Do they have funny as well as sad stories about school and growing up? Were there mentors and heroes? Good.

But if the stories are of pain, or challenges, or if their faces go hard and cold, their voices go quiet or loud and monotone in either way, and most importantly if there are no stories at all?

Caveat Emptor, Ladies. Caveat Emptor.

Swipe, Swap, Swope

Dating is different from when I was in the game. You saw someone you liked, you did what you could to catch their eye. Did they look interested? Then you made small talk. Was the small talk flirtatious?

And so it went and the relationship evolved as it would.

But has dating really changed that much? In my day, if no one local interested you, you put an ad in any of various flyers or magazines. Want a large reach? Use a magazine which has a large market. Want a more local reach but wider than you physically have? Use a smaller, city-wide or county-wide flyer.

Whichever market you wanted, you wrote something you hoped was witty, engaging, and enticing, something which let readers know enough about you to make a decision to reach out or not. You could include a picture if you were wealthy or didn't care about the price (printing costs were prohibitive!) and few did.

Now a world of dating possibilities is a mobile away. Like what you see? Swap. Don't like what you see? Swipe. Not sure about what you see? Swope.

A friend of mine, Karen, finds herself in the dating game once again. We got to talking about the various dating apps and sites she's tried, the profiles she's looked through and tapped or clicked.

At one point we got together and she called up some profiles They seemed normal to me. I mean, I wasn't seeing any red flags. Then she began translating the acronyms (like NSA meaning No Strings Attached) along with the profiles as a whole. I'd offer that she was harsh and recognized that her harshness came from experience. It was a defense mechanism based on responding to some profiles and meeting some people.

I noted that she was only showing me text-based profiles or profiles with "your pix gets mine" in one form or another. "What about the video sites?"

"Same thing. There are people now who make a living by making you look good on video dating sites. And that's not even counting the AI generated profiles."

"You're kidding."

No, she wasn't. Slightly stunned, I asked some friends about their experiences and shared some of Karen's. I was curious to know if this was a female-only response and it wasn't. Some of my male friends shared their experiences and it turned out, yes, the door swung both ways.

So I asked both men and women to show me profiles they felt were "honest" — a "What You See Is What You Get" in online dating — profiles that provided a good enough idea of the person to move forward. I didn't care if they would actually respond, just wanted to know if they felt the person was honest about who they were, what they wanted, and so on.

As always, it comes down to some simple rules:

1. Be honest when you write the ad.
2. Be honest in what you're really looking for when answering an ad.

Everyone I talked with said it differently and they all said the same thing. If you're looking for someone simply as a social partner (you like to go dancing, want to go with someone but don't want to be involved beyond that, for example) make sure you state that clearly. Keeping expectations in place is crucial.

State your limitations and expectations early. Few things irritated males and females more than having a great online experience degrade to a horrible offline experience. Most of the time people's core beliefs, limitations and expectations come out in email and phone calls, sometimes they don't and that's when troubles arise. Both genders said learning limitations and expectations early saved them time and torment.

Ask around to learn who's playing you and who's serious. In an excellent example of protective social behavior, I learned that many of these sites have communities in which women (for example) share their experiences. One of the great outgrowths of this is that certain males are quickly identified as "risky bets" and more importantly, why. But women, be equally advised, men are learning from you and have started the same mutual support systems. Women who are deemed as predatory or risky are also recognized and commented on.

In case you aren't sure, the three basic rules for good social behavior anywhere are:

1. Be honest about yourself with others
2. State your needs and wants clearly
3. Ask your peers when you're not sure.

And may you find what your heart's (and mind's) desire.

(and with great thanks to Karen, Maria, Dave, Marcie, Ned and Jonny)

Sex on the Beach

Anybody remember those first school dances you went to? The boys lined up on one wall, the girls on the other? And remember that the boys gathered in groups of maybe 2-3 and the girls in groups of 5 or more?

What you're observing is a proto-typical gender behavior bias. That's a $25 way of saying men and women behave differently. Kind of like noticing that wolves go after the most vulnerable member of a herd or that the bull elk challenges all competitors to his harem. It's all obvious when you know what you're looking at.

For example, somewhere up around the 4m45s mark in a presentation I gave on Gender Specific Marketing Discoveries, I comment on the fact that men sat singularly or in groups of 1-3 on one side of the room and the women clustered in noticeably larger groups on the other side of the room. A solitary male is the usual case with males over 30 years old (they tend to have more confidence whether they should or not).

What it all comes down to sex on the beach. Humans, despite what some might like to think, carry in their genes all the behaviors that helped us climb from the primordial muck to where we are today. Everything that worked is in there. One of the things that worked for males was separating themselves from other males so that females could individualize them, get a better look at them, could evaluate them better, get a good fix on their potentials as mates and providers.

In short, males establish territories. Those nature documentaries about seals on the beach have it correct. It's amusing to watch several million years of evolutionary wiring go into conflict with a few thousand years of human civilization, especially when you recognize that much of what we call "civilization" is designed to deal with all that nasty evolutionary wiring.

Anthropologists recognize ceremonies and rituals. Ceremonies rarely change because they define us as a species. Rituals constantly change because they define us as a group, a tribe, a family, a religion, a sect, a nationality, a people.

You've probably heard the term "mating ritual". That first, awkward school dance is a mating ritual. Its purpose is for kids to have fun, yes, and also to have them learn how to evaluate members of the opposite sex, also known as partner selection and a mating ritual in disguise. That school dance is an example of socially acceptable behavior meeting evolutionary wiring big time. Another example of the difference between ceremony and ritual is marriage. The ritual of marriage varies from culture to culture but the ceremony of marriage — the "this-person-that-person" thing — is pretty well established in our species.

What's more interesting is observing the individuals who've made accommodations so that their evolutionary wiring and social training work hand in hand, or don't.

For example, an adult male who always seeks the company of his male peers probably won't be a good choice for mate or provider. An adult male who is comfortable by himself and will spend time with male peers is better. An adult male who can be by himself in a social setting (a bar, a dance, a beach), who intentionally catches your eye without intruding on what you're doing and quickly (but graciously) acknowledges your interest or lack thereof? Learn his name. He's probably worth it.

Men, what about women who traverse social training and evolutionary wiring? Interestingly enough the same rules apply. If they're comfortable with themselves, recognize social signals as they are intended and don't dispute them, ask for their name. Talk and do remember to listen. They probably have a lot to tell you.

Sing Me a Little Song

I wrote about the importance of sound in the mating game in "I Love the Way You Say That". That dealt with how women could determine if a potential partner was going to work out based on the sound of their voice.

It turns out the same is true for men, although it takes a slightly different turn. It's not so much the sound of their voice, it's whether or not they sing. Or hum. I think laughter qualifies, too. It turns out that part of the male's mental wiring is to determine life-partner value and worth by sound. This happens all the time in the animal world. Everything from mosquitoes to elephants hum, sing, or otherwise make sounds that attract each other. TV documentaries tend to focus on the mating calls of the males and it is also true that males are drawn to the mating sounds of females. This starts in the womb. Newborns of either sex respond quicker to a female voice than a male's, and the trait carries for males into adulthood (amusing anecdote: some home alarm companies have their alarms announce with a warm, female voice rather than a harsh alarm sound. Turns out people respond quicker and more actively. Especially if they're asleep.

Kind of like momma calling you to dinner when you nap, I guess).

How do humans do it?

Men like to hear their partners laugh, sing, hum...forgive the possible stereotype, but anything but talk. Talking involves different parts of the brain and we use our voices differently when we talk than when we vocalize in any other way.

As noted above, males are attracted to the sounds of laughter, singing, and humming beginning in the womb, when they were babes in their mothers' arms, and continues throughout their lives. Most mothers (and this is cross-cultural) make very distinct laughing, singing and humming sounds with their children, not talking (as in "conversation") with them until the child is ambulatory (meaning "they can get around on their own. You don't need to carry them everywhere").

So guys, does your potential partner sing or hum or laugh (and not just at your jokes)? And do you like it? Even better, does his or her voice sound like music to your ears? Congrats, you've got a keeper.

Why Did I Get All the Girls?

Male friends in college were often envious of my abilities with the womens. It was not uncommon to hear comments such as "How do you rate?", "I knew you'd know her" and some less respectable phrases. Even after Susan and I got together women had no problem sharing their intimacies with me, the secrets they'd normally only share with other women, seeking me out for this or that. Fortunately I'm amazingly dense and Susan usually has to let me know when girltalk becomes flirting (too much of an anthropologist, me).

What makes me so attractive to women? In a word, I'm average. It turns out that while men will flock to a pretty face, women will flock to what's average. So what do I mean by flock? The reward circuits in the female brain are activated by what is normal, what is visually average. The male reward circuitry fires more readily for the visually ... umm ... distinctive(?). My average features, it seems, are positive signals to women according to studies conducted at Harvard Medical School and Massachusetts General Hospital. I'll admit that while this finding explains a lot (to me, personally), it seems to go against evolutionary law (choosing mates for survival and beneficial traits, etc.). Women should choose according to those same evolutionary laws. And it turns out they do, if your brain is wired female.

NextStage's research has repeatedly demonstrated that women favor rewards that continually provide benefit over time, not all at once (as opposed to males and if this isn't a statement about reproductive biology affecting neurology or vice versa nothing is). An average-looking male — provided other beneficial traits are demonstrated — satisfies those long-term benefit and goal requirements that are deep inside the female brain. What are those other beneficial traits? Being able to listen, to respond appropriately, to share, ... It comes down to a lesson women have known for centuries — know when to be male and when to be female. More accurately, know when to demonstrate maleness and when to demonstrate femaleness.

A male's ability to learn that lesson goes back to how males and females define social networks and community — men create hierarchical (or vertical) networks, women create horizontal (or latitudinal) networks. Women will create and participate in hierarchical networks and usually some form of achievement or advancement is the intention. Men will create and participate in horizontal networks albeit (often) unwillingly until certain safety signals are demonstrated and maintained. Gender differences in community are also interesting to study. Most male communities form outside of the home (i.e., they go someplace to meet), most female communities form inside the home (they meet at a community member's house and often move from house to house so the burden is shared equally).

Why so? A male inviting another male into their private space (home) is a demonstration of power and authority in the male psyche, hence meetings are done in neutral territories to demonstrate safety. The metaphor "bearding the lion in his den", i.e., controlling or confronting an adversary in their own territory, is one of the ways this concept shows up in language (note the use of "his"? We'd never beard the lion in *her* den). Women, however, view home as safe and secure (in most cases) so a woman inviting others into her home is a true sign of acceptance, an ability to share whatever bounty they have with others.

Where these lines don't overlap well is in modern business settings. A male can call a subordinate male into his office and reprimand him then both males will (usually) go about their business. A female calling a subordinate female into her office is a woman breaking the rules and (again, usually) some form of rebonding needs to take place.

Males wanting to traverse gender boundaries without thought or concern need to remember what one of my female friends once told one of her female friends about me, "You don't have to worry about Joseph. He's not really a guy." What was being said was the females' ability to recognize guys versus men. This brings us back to knowing when to demonstrate maleness and femaleness.

You always want women to recognize you as a male, you rarely (if ever) want them to think of you as just another guy.

Short People
... Or Short Men, At Least

There is, sorry to share, some truth to the dictum that short males don't get as many dates as their taller peers. I'm reminded of the MASH episode in which Radar buys lifts for his shoes so he'll be more appealing to the women of the 4077th. And while I do not know any males who've had themselves surgically enhanced height-wise, I do know such methods exist.

So, is it a truism that women prefer taller men?

It is from an evolutionary standpoint. It goes back to something I often mention in my marketing classes and trainings: size equals power. In the evolutionary sense, a tall male regardless of any other morphological tendencies must be more powerful — hence a better provider, protector, etc. — than a shorter male with the same morphological tendencies.

And there have been numerous studies demonstrating that taller males do better academically, socially, healthwise, businesswise, financially, economically, ...

But the question is...

The question is "Is there something about the genetic coding for male tallness that also increases their other skills or do we as prisoners of our neurobiology allow tall males more do-overs than we allow shorter males?"

Ah, now that's a question.

It is true that less reproductively successful males (in the vernacular "unlucky") are significantly shorter than males with children. This is true across all age groups save one, males born in the late 1920s - early 1930s. Why so?

Because males born in that 7-10 year timespan were getting married and actively reproducing right at the end of WWII. There were lots more women than there were men. There was an (ahem) shortage of males so short males were more reproductively successful as a group than short males of other generations.

Notice that I skirted around that "prisoners of neurobiology" thing?

What should shorter men do about this? It's really quite simple. Find a partner who values the inner you, who looks beyond the surface, who will see you as a person instead of an object.

If you're not sure how to do this, read Rostand's *Cyrano de Bergerac* or watch a more recent version, Steve Martin's *Roxanne*. Your final out is to ask women. They're used to screening partners who select for physical features all the time. Go ahead. I dare you to say, "All you care about is looks!"

And that prisoners thing? Let's talk about that at a conference. Sitting down.

Duetting
Part 1

I've written a few times about how sound affects relationships, specifically the sounds our partners and possible partners make and how our conscious and non-conscious responses to those sounds make and break relationships.

The latest piece of research I'll share is (to me) a logical outcome of what we've studied previously: partners who sing together — what's called duetting — tend to have stronger relationships than partners who only talk to each other.

Remember, talking is extremely important. It's just that couples who duet — not professionally, not in front of audiences, simply when they're together and it doesn't matter if it's in private or public — tend to bond at much deeper levels than their less euterpic peers.

The reason duetting adds to relationship bonds is because (as noted previously) it engages different parts of the brain, more primitive parts of the brain (from an evolutionary perspective, that is). Most people recognize that music is often part of romantic exchanges. When people say something like "They're playing our song", they're stating that a very strong memory-emotion-cognition bond has been formed and the music is triggering those very different parts of the brain to synchronize — to fire together, as it were — in response. This kind of triggering is called an "anchor" and the term is used similarly in many psychologic, social, anthropologic, and neuro-logic disciplines.

Humans who duet are performing an extremely old evolutionary function. Much like howling wolves, trumpeting elephants, singing whales, calling apes and all the rest, we are creating synchrony between ourselves and someone else. This is an extremely important social function at the most intimate social level — we're finding out that we're loved, accepted, honored, ..., at a very deep level.

This is social bonding, pack bonding, group bonding at its most primitive, when we first huddled together under the stars and dozed — we couldn't afford to fall asleep with all the predators around — on the vast grasslands.

In short, duetting lets us know we are safe with each other, that the other literally "has our back".

So the next time you're alone with your special other, ask them to hum a little with you. Or sing, even better. Interestingly, reciting poetry together often serves the same purpose.

Give them time if they're hesitant. And remember to laugh. Especially when you're the one who's offkey.

Duetting
Part 2

I study ethology.

I know. You're surprised.

"What? Joseph studies? What's the world coming to?"

Specifically, behavioral ethology (feel free to repeat the above).

More simply, I study animal behavior and for several reasons. Various animals are used as human surrogates in research (I understand this and don't like it). My interest is in animal models of human behavior, meaning "What can we learn about ourselves by observing animals, and matching their behavioral patterns to our own?" This is something I've written about many times. You can see animal examples of human behavior in mating behaviors, group dynamics, family patterns, ...

Take *Pheugopedius euophrys* (aka plain-tailed wrens). Females and males cooperate to produce a duet song in which both sexes rapidly alternate singing syllables. That's a behavioral ethologist's way of saying "They each sing a lyric, join together on the chorus, and so it goes until the song's done."

Isn't it great how scientists can make the perfectly understandable oblique and confusing?

I wrote previously about the power of duetting and creating strong relationships. We also learned from animal studies partners who don't duet tend to have less stable relationships.

But Joseph, we don't sing together. Is our relationship doomed?

No, not necessarily. It turns out duetting applies to all communications, not just singing. Take conversations. Does one listen while the other talks? Does the other listen while one talks?

Excellent! You're duetting without notes getting in the way.

Oh, but they are! Did you know conversations have rhythmic patterns? Or that voice pitch is likened to notes on a scale? Or that emphasizing certain words over others is likened to musical emphasis - *forte, mezzo forte,* and so on - on certain notes or musical measures?

Those rhythmic patterns - the emphasis placed on specific syllables and words, the length of sentences, the choice of words - are based on duetting behavior. Ditto pitch, ditto emphasis, ditto... Psycho- and socio- and neural-linguists know the difference between the words themselves and how they're spoken as digital - the words themselves - and analog - how they're spoken.

I know you'll be shocked - Shocked, I tell you! - that the analog signal often carries more information than the digital, meaning how something is said is often more important than the words themselves.

And it doesn't matter if it's two life-partners, employer and employee, friends, lovers, parent and child, ... Duetting is there, get used to it.

Back to it

Does one interrupt the other? Bad duetting. Somebody's going to look for another nest. They might not do it physically, but emotionally, psychologically, and/or spiritually they will.

And where the mind goes, the body will follow.

Do you finish each other's sentences and laugh about it? Congrats! That's more involved duetting. It's an evolutionary signal we've chosen partners correctly, that we're so comfortable with each other's knowledge of ourselves we can appreciate their knowledge and use that mutual appreciation to grow stronger together.

Let's apply animal studies to disagreements. Do temperatures rise, emotions flare, words become harsh, possibly abusive, do the partners talk over each other as if counting *ku*, not letting each other respond? Do they talk to opposite purposes, talking simultaneously but neither listening to the other? Bad duetting there.

What if disagreements are reasoned, each partner working to understand the other's point of view without correction? Asking for clarification is fine; it shows we're paying attention, and again, not to correct, only to understand. Behavioral and neurophysiological studies of duetting partners - especially during disagreements - demonstrate listening partners are more aware of the emotional energy as well as the psychological energy behind the words, meaning they respond to what's being felt beyond what's being said.

What does that mean? It means duetting partners - even in disagreements - address the root of the disagreement. They'll listen to the surface and look for what's underneath, the root cause, if you will, and focus the discussion there.

One more thing we learn from animal studies, and something which goes against modern cultural norms: disagreements initiated by women tend to resolve more easily than those initiated by men. It would be nice if one could pin this down to neural morphology and such doesn't address much if any at all of the issue. Alas, it is a cultural issue. Women, despite our enlightenment (and more and more I fear due to our increasing disenlightenment) are still second-class citizens. They are the greatest (numerically) group of second-class citizens in western culture, and their ability to interact with men as equals exists as a hysteresis loop of fascinating fluctuations. As a friend's great aunt admonished the women in her family, "Feel free to swim, my darling daughters — just don't go near the water."

Guys, Size Matters!
But You'll Never Guess Where

Research going back to 2003 indicates that women are attracted to men based on the size of their... ...teeth.

Teeth? You've got to be kidding, right?

In one of the most interesting pieces of research I've seen to date on why shes favor hes, it seems that a strong, non-conscious factor in what draws women into relationships with men is the size, shape, color and general health of their teeth.

Is that all that attracts them? Of course not. Koinophology and koinophilia — the science of what we find beautiful/attractive and why — is one of the oldest areas of study yet one of the youngest fields of science around, and I've done week-long seminars and trainings on how to use human images and images of body parts in marketing based on what we've learned starting with cave drawings and pottery shards to the present.

That offered, women respond more favorably to men who smile than men who don't (duh!) but the smile has to have certain characteristics. A true smile is done with the eyes, not just the mouth and cheeks, and the expression "he has a smile that lights up his face" is an indication of just how much change there can be in a true smile versus a wan-smile (the smile we give to be polite or even to show tolerance of a remark, etc.). Readers with a knowledge of primate ethology know when a smile is a smile is a smile, especially if you've worked with the higher primates, and most domesticated aid animals (dogs, birds, monkeys) know when a smile is right and true and will hiss, bark, or spit when the smile ain't.

Then there's a healthy, even display of teeth. Nothing too prominent, no underbites or overbites and so on (moderate overbites are a recent feature to our species and only occur in modern cultures). Nice, white teeth are always a plus (I guess all those toothpaste commercials were correct after all). And evenness counts much more than size (to a certain degree, neither too large nor too small is best).

I'm guessing this is a very old evolutionary holdover. We now know that healthy, strong teeth are a primary indicator of overall physical health and fitness (did you know there are some venereal diseases that make their first appearance in the teeth and gums?). Males with the best, strongest teeth were by definition the fittest mates.

So brush 'em up, guys, and let them see you smile.

By the way and before I forget, moderate overbites are becoming the norm for modern humans in modern societies because we use knives, forks, and such to get food into our mouths, meaning we no longer tear meat off the bone or use our incisors to get a piece of food off the whole. The next time you bite into a nice, juicy apple (or anything hard which fits in your hand), take a moment to note you line up your bottom and top incisors a bit more than usual. People raised completely on processed foods never do that. There's no need. Most processed foods are soft enough to be directly palatable. Which is also why people raised exclusively on processed foods often require more dental care than those raised on fresh fruits and vegetables.

Ah, evolution. We've done you proud.

And while we're talking evolution, a bit of panspecies advice: never *ever* **ever** smile and look directly at a male silverback gorilla. Or any higher primate. They will focus on the display of teeth because the massive musculature needed to power those massive jaws makes facial expressions above the mouth too challenging to do except in extreme cases. A genuine human smile is a challenge/threat to them, even when we engage our eyes. Primates can only do that when there's an extreme reason to do so.

Like they're being threatened.

Or challenged.

So don't.

Women Leave the Dance

Long, long ago (I was in 8th grade) I went to a YMCA dance with some friends. Kids from all over my hometown went and most of us tended to hang out with the kids from our own schools.

I still remember one boy I didn't know who wanted to dance with Linda Greenstreet. Phil Llewellyn was dancing with her. This other boy pushed Phil (who was a big, strong but gentle lad) away from Linda. He didn't ask if he could cut in, he pushed Phil hard then put his fists up.

Naturally, all of Phil's friends circled this intruder. Linda and a bunch of the other girls from my school huddled together and talked (no idea what they said). Linda said out loud that it was okay, she'd dance with this newcomer.

His dance, more than anything else, is what causes me to remember this incident. Even in 8th grade I recognized it as a territorial display. I didn't know the term but knew the dance — a large step with hands up not quite in fists, a facial grimace with eyes wide open and watching all the other males in our group, and an almost perfect square with Linda essentially dancing by herself at its center — was a demonstration of male dominance and possession. Years later, remembering his steps and posture, I was saddened to think of what his family life must have been like.

In any case, after that dance was over the girls from my school and several others mysteriously disappeared. I did find out that while Linda danced the other girls called parents to come get them.

This one fellow through his efforts alone closed the dance down.

Interestingly enough, research now has social models of the hyperaggressive male and sure enough, one overly aggressive male zeroes out the dating possibilities for all of us. Females avoid all males, not just the hyperaggressive one, because they know the most likely outcome of such encounters is that everyone gets harmed.

Also interesting is that females will tolerate lots of aggressive males together but there is a limit that any one male can go in their aggression before the shutdown occurs. What this point is is unknown in the large and obvious in the small.

Go to a party and if you start seeing the women congregate by themselves, directing mutual glances at one or two specific males, you're seeing the shutdown start. Do the women's movements become smaller, perhaps tighter, more collected (if you've studied equine management you'll know what I mean. Normal movements are now performed in a smaller space)? Then things are escalating. Do the women start pulling themselves out of the center of the room or gathering area? Are they making motions to leave en masse? Then it's obvious.

Guys, follow the women's lead. Hyperaggressive males are dealing with issues well outside the scope of what the immediate social gathering entails and there's very little you can do – well-intentioned or otherwise — to make things flow more easily. Following the women's lead eventually leaves the hyperaggressive male all alone in the center of the room. That happens often enough and they might get the message.

Besides, if you follow the women's lead you'll be in the parking lot — or wherever — when they head for their cars. Talk to them, ask them if they're okay, say you're sorry about that jerk dancing a huge square in the middle of the room.

Nice guys may finish last but at least they do get to finish what they started.

Good Partners and Family Size

It seems there's an interesting correlation between family size and longevity of relationships. I haven't read on this in detail so I'm not prepared to comment in detail, and it seems that people who create long-term, long-lasting partners come from larger families of origin.

In one way, this makes sense. Someone coming from a family that stays together long enough to produce several offspring is being given a model of relational longevity.

But there's so much data contrary to that (mostly cultural) that it's a hard one for me to accept.

The core of this research is that people raised in larger families acquire more social skills, more interpersonal skills, more communication skills, ... basically they get more acculturation and societalization so they're better able to cope with the normal life stresses and strains that occur in partnering situations.

That completely makes sense.

It especially makes sense if you do a pancultural study. Take into account societies around the world, first through fourth world, and it makes more and more sense. Isolate the study to just the US and I think (this is a guess, I haven't studied this in detail) it fails.

Still, it is an interesting data point for people wondering if their current special someone is going to be a good long-term, possibly lifetime special someone: ask to meet their family.

Do you find yourself walking into a tribal meeting? Are there a choir of voices around the kitchen table or in the living room? Are there so many people that you can't help bumping into each other and when you do is there laughter or territorial displays?

You never know. It could make a difference down the road.

Dangerous - Or at least "Dominant" or "Domineering" - Women

I'm just betting that title will get attention. Let me explain what I mean: this chapter will be about women with strong personalities. Males have various terms for such women.

No, that's not correct, either. Let me have another go at this. I mean, my wife has a strong personality and is not dangerous, dominant, domineering or any other negative term that some males might apply to her.

Ah...how about women lacking good personal boundaries who demonstrate their lack of good personal boundaries via aggressive or unnecessarily assertive behavior?

Yeah, that's better. But I'd never get any readers with "Women Lacking Good Personal Boundaries Who Demonstrate Their Lack of Good Personal Boundaries via Aggressive Or Unnecessarily Assertive Behavior", don't you think?

So what about such women?

Well, friends, they're dangerous. Allow me to be an evolutionary biologist for a few sentences. Having poor personal boundaries is not a survival trait. Anybody who blindly counts on the kindness of strangers is going to encounter some very strange acts of "kindness." But what if a negative survival trait such as having poor personal boundaries is intimately linked to a very positive survival trait, something like being an incredible cook?

The poor personal boundaries will make you want to cook for everybody whenever they want, whatever they want. Being an incredible cook will make others want to keep you around (alive) to cook for them.

(Yes, I know it's a stretch. It's an example, okay? And enough evolutionary biology for now)

Having poor personal boundaries is an indication of many psychological challenges, most of them not helpful in daily living. Such people can be anything from minor annoyances to requiring restraining orders. How are poor personal boundaries demonstrated?

There are lots of ways. Someone who eats your food without asking, someone who goes through your things without asking, someone who wears your clothes without asking, blah blah blah without asking.

Asking permission to do something is probably the most obvious demonstration of personal boundaries in today's society. It is a demonstration of respect for person and property.

And what about the Aggressive/Assertive Woman?

First, being assertive — asking for what you want, stating your needs, etc. — is fine. In fact, it's pretty much required for healthy psychologies. Being aggressive is not fine and is not required for healthy psychologies.

A woman who states her wants and needs and will accept your limits in meeting them, my Brothers, is a keeper. Look no further, you've got one of the good ones.

A woman who states her wants and needs and becomes increasingly militant when you're unable to meet them? Stay away, Brothers, there are others who will accept your limits and help you exceed them.

By the way, Sisters, the reverse is true, too. The man who accepts your personal boundaries is the one you want. The fellow who demands more and more and more? Not the one for you, methinks. Don't even try to fix him. All that will happen is that you'll break down and he'll go off to another.

You Smell Funny

Perfumers and associated industries spend an incredible amount of money producing various scents for our use. Deodorants mask the caucasian from smelling like goats (for example. And I'm not kidding about the goat smell, either).

Some people appreciate that there's only one scent/perfume/olfactory mask they can wear and all others make their scent foul. I'm one of those lucky ones. I can only wear musk-based scents. Wear any others and I quickly clear rooms.

Ah, the joys of individual body chemistries.

And that brings us directly to this chapter's topic: how do you pick a scent that will be pleasing both to you and to those you want to please? Pleasing perfumes, deodorants and their kin evolved from what we once called love potions. We would go to our village wisewoman and she would ask who we wanted to have fall in love with us, when we would see them next, and whether others would be present. You'll find this mix of questions in fairy and folk tales from around the world and with good reason.

What pleases us olfactively and vomeronasally (collectively "our sense of smell". Don't worry if you've never heard of your vomeronasal sense. Nobody knew it existed until the late 1990s.) is first based on our common biologies — we are designed to like certain scents and not others, then on our family's preferences, then on our culture's, and then on our society's as a whole.

Our olfactory senses are among the most primitive. The only older sensory system our bodies have is also the most dominant: our sense of touch. Our whole body is devoted to our sense of touch and even our other senses yield to it. This is why it hurts when we poke ourselves in the eye. Why should it hurt? Why not just go blind for a moment or two? Because our sense of touch signals the eye is damaged before our sense of sight signals "Cover Your Eyes!"

Because olfaction is one of the oldest it often goes unnoticed by most people until there's a really good smell or a really bad smell wafting towards us. Does the smell of freshly baked bread or frying garlic or apple pie cooling or pot roast cooking or bao steaming make your stomach growl? Or maybe just the thought of those things?

Congratulations, you've just noticed one evolutionary purpose of our sense of smell — to find good things to eat.

Likewise does the smell of a ripe horse or cow field cause a hasty retreat? Excellent, that's another of its evolutionary purposes — to keep us out of nasty environments and situations.

And both of these grew out of our sense of smell's original purpose — finding us someone to love.

That's where the wisewoman's questions come in. Did we want everybody to fall in love with us or just one person (and if personal genome sequencing kits ever come to WalMart®, be careful)? Was this someone from our village or another village? When would we see them?

The last question deals with dispersal method. Do we ingest it so that we carry that magical scent through our pores (it takes a while) or apply it topically so that our body heat activates it (fairly rapid)?

The second question deals with those things we smelled as babies and growing up and have long forgotten. Just as there are comfort foods so there are comfort smells. Knowing where someone is from answers this.

The first question tells us the type of scent required: animal, vegetable or mineral.

The wisewoman's questions are the same one perfumers deal with today. Much more scientifically, of course.

And usually with far worse results.

So the next time you're considering which $500 bottle of perfume or aftershave to purchase for that special occasion, consider whom you're wanting to entice. If you know enough about them you might be just as well off with some bread, wine, cheese and a scent of some vegetable, fruit, or flower in your hair.

Appropriate Dress

On average, who spends more time on buying clothes, accessorizing them, and staring at their reflection to make sure everything is on just right, men or women?

This isn't an easy one so take your time with it.

And while we're at it, let's up the ante — will an individual spend more time looking good when they're out with friends or out looking for a mate? Let's start with whether women or men spend more time dressing and buying. If you guessed that it's about equal, you're correct.

Myself, I answered "women" then held up my hand. "Let me think about this," I said.

And think I did.

Clothing is one of the most obvious and immediate demonstrations of group identity, cultural identity, ethnic identity, social class, peer recognition, ... (I cover much of this in Reading Virtual Minds Volume I: Science and History, fyi). It turns out that if you measure across the broadest spectrum possible, men and women spend equal amounts of time making sure they look just right with men leading the mirror charge as economic groups go higher and higher.

And if they want to climb an economic or social ladder, watch out. Did you think John Travolta's Tony Manero character spent all that time on his hair just for kicks?

It's a pretty interesting study, the science of ornamentation, dressing and such. Anthropologists and archaeologists spend lots of time studying such things because they reveal so much about cultures, peoples, and most of all, mating habits.

That last part leads us to whether people spend more time pruning and preening when they're out with friends or out mate-hunting. If you guessed people will spend more time preparing for a night out with their friends than out looking for a mate, good for you, you got it.

Women going out with the girls for a night on the town have an acute if nonconscious sense of peer group pressure and hearing "I love what that dress/blouse/skirt/... does for you" is enough to make the night grand. Likewise, men will compliment each other's appearance, if not with outright statements then with reflective comments such as "That woman over there thinks you're hot."

Arguing in Public

I'll make it simple. Don't do it. Ever.

Let me amplify. Don't start an argument in public. You may win the argument, however everyone around you will think you're a poot. "Poot" is a technical term, I know, and I think you get the idea. Everyone witnessing or hearing the argument will side with the individual who didn't start the argument. Depending on who's around you when the argument is started, this can be either a plus or a minus. It turns out that society (and it doesn't seem to matter what society) likes things to remain calm, quiet, and basically uninteresting. A little excitement is good in private and sometimes in public, but only when the excitees are prepared and know going in that excitement is going to be the outcome. This is why we have amusement parks, scary rides, bungee jumping, so on and so forth.

However, an unprecedented excitement? No thanks. Uh-uh. No, nyet, nada.

So let's say you and someone else are out in public somewhere. You're shopping, walking, whatever. One of you starts an argument.

Okay, what do I mean by "argument". An argument occurs when there's no give-and-take, no consideration for the other person's point of view or feelings, when the subject under discussion was above and beyond the control of arguee, when the arguer uses personally abusive language, threatens violence, when the arguee indicates they don't want to take part in the conversation and the arguer won't stop, ... pick any bad thing you want, when it happens it's an argument, neither discussion nor conversation could it be.

Two people reasoning through things, accepting and acknowledging each other's emotional biases, both arguer and arguee understanding that logic may not apply, allowing each other to state their case or understand that words may fail, ... these are discussions between loving and caring individuals. Ask them if they're having an argument and they'd probably say no, they were just getting something out of their system, clearing their mind, voicing a concern, asking for support, what have you.

But an argument? The public trust has been violated. It won't matter how valid an argument is, the arguer will be held responsible for violating that trust and held accountable.

Have you ever seen an argument start and someone say, "Hey, take it outside, okay?"

What's really being stated is "Take that argument away from me, so far away that I do not have to worry that the aggression demonstrated might become physically demonstrated and hence a personal threat."

So first suggestion, don't argue, period.

Second suggestion, if you must, discuss things when both arguer and arguee are prepared and willing to listen, to support each other and not count ku or say wounding things to each other in some kind of emotional tit-for-tat ping-pong match.

Remember, we're here to help each other, not hurt. Our purpose on this planet is to help each other get home, nothing more, nothing less.

Poisoning Pigeons in the Park

Some readers may remember the Tom Lehrer song by that name. In case you don't, you can enjoy it on YouTube.

Dr. Ruth, a NextStageologist of long standing (*see Appendix: Definitions for more context -ed.*), and I often sing it when we're together. Most people don't know that Tom Lehrer started out as a brilliant mathematician. He got into music when he realized he could make more money with his catchy melodies and humorous lyrics than by calculating $\cdot\blacktriangledown$ functions such as

$$u\cdot\blacktriangledown = u_r\partial_r + u_\varphi(1/r)\partial_\varphi + u_z\partial_z$$

This isn't about Tom Lehrer per se, except that in writing this chapter he came to mind and I love to share.

It's about pigeons, men, and listening to women talk about them. Susan and I were having lunch at an outdoor cafe that bordered a park recently. We were watching two female and one male pigeon. The male fluttered down between the two females and some crumbs someone threw down to them. The male began strutting, puffing, cooing, and doing all the usual things males do when they want to convince a female they're the right stuff.

No matter what the females did to get to the breadcrumbs, the male got in their way, strutted, puffed, and cooed. Finally one female took off and the male upped his ante with the remaining female, pretty much chasing her around the crumbs so she never had a chance to enjoy them.

And then she took off.

Meanwhile some other pigeons had landed and were enjoying the crumbs.

While this went on, one of the things that got Susan and I chuckling was overhearing three mid-20s women at the next table give a play-by-play of "Pigeon Love". It was hilarious. I almost blew espresso out my nose at one point.

I looked up after the pigeons left to congratulate the women on their analysis and stopped cold. I motioned Susan to look at the women. They were continuing their analysis.

They weren't looking at the pigeons at all. They were looking at some people by the bar. Their sympathies (and ours, as we watched) went to some peer-aged women who were doing their best to signal a persistent young man they weren't interested. Our near-table analysts were clearly saying, "Give it up. God, just give it up!"

Why this fellow wasn't getting the message...well, he probably was. There's an aspect of the male psyche that goes "When people are watching, you can't give up. Ever. And if you do, it must be on your terms" (this is a big thing in politics. Nobody can "lose face" when political exchanges run foul).

So this fellow was looking for a way out, a way that made it look like he was on top of the situation for any of us watching.

And finally it came. A friend (this other fellow really was a friend) at the other end of the bar chatting with some people was also watching. He called out, got the "I can't give up now" male's attention, then walked over, drink in hand. "Bill? I haven't seen you in months!" He interrupted the pattern, even asked the women if he could pull Bill away, then guided Bill to the far side of the bar.

The women at the bar were visibly relieved. Our near-table analysts — they were becoming quite agitated by the display — were also visibly relieved (I think they were going to congratulate the women at the bar for getting out of the situation). Bill, the bull-pigeon who didn't realize the females had psychologically flown away, was confused.

His friend...Susan called our waiter over, said to give Bill's friend another of whatever he was drinking and add it to our tab, and tell him, "Nicely played."

He raised his glass to us on our way out.

Sometimes you really want to just poison those pigeons, you know? It's like a mercy killing.

Make Her Laugh

Okay guys...you're in a bar or restaurant or the office or in the grocery store or wherever. You see an attractive woman who you want to meet and are having a severe attack of ice-breaker-itis (known to some as pickup-line-itis and chatup-line-itis).

Let's say you're in the grocery store. She's carrying a basket, not pushing a cart and you oh-so-carefully glance in and notice there's Swanson Dinner's-For-One, a couple of apples and not a dozen, a small bag of grapes and not a bunch, a quart of skim milk and not a gallon. Okay, good, she's probably single.

A can of tuna fish...no, wait...a can of cat food. No, two cans. Okay, she has a cat. Even better, you love cats.

You want to introduce yourself and she's heard so many pickup lines before and you've never been great at this, what to do, what to say? According to studies done in the US and Canada, make her laugh. A good sense of humor signals several important mate selection factors — mental health, intelligence, creativity — to the human female.

And it gets better. A good sense of humor cuts across all ethnic, cultural, etc., boundaries. Making someone laugh is considered both a prosocial and survival ability regardless of who's doing it and who the audience is.

But there are some rules...

The ability to bring a moment of laughter, of joy, or happiness is definitely an attractor to women across all cultures, but there are some rules about the kind of humor that also cut across all those boundaries, as well.

For example, sarcasm is not a form of humor that engenders the opposite gender. Don Rickles is funny when he's on stage and everybody knows what to expect. He's not funny when the two of you are strolling through a mall and he's randomly insulting people walking past you.

Vulgarity is also not a good ice-breaking humor style. Interestingly, if the woman makes a vulgar remark it's often to test the male, to determine what the male's real objectives are and real sense of style, so be careful with this one.

Self-deprecating humor is good and only in moderation. A self-deprecating joke or two is enough, then move on to other topics quickly.

Steve Martin Does It Right

One thing that works and does so across all cultures is what's called "theater of the absurd". Steve Martin seems to have a good handle on this as several males interviewed referenced him as the inspiration for some of their most successful ice-breaking lines. One fellow noticed a box of dogbones in a woman's shopping cart, quickly went to a costume store in the mall and purchased a pair of eyeglasses but instead of a "Groucho" face this pair had fluffy dog ears and a nose attached, raced back into the grocery store, found the woman, walked up to her and said in a conspiratorial tone, "Woof."

"She laughed all over the frozen chicken," he commented when asked about his success. "We've been together eight years now and she still says she loves me because I make her laugh."

So, guys...make her laugh.

Men Get Stupid Over Sex

I've been laughing my head off over some recent research findings. I'm laughing because the research is...well...funny to me. Kind of like certain types of comedy. Some forms of comedy derive their power by demonstrating our own foolishness. We're actually laughing at ourselves through the safety of the comedy.

So it was with this research. My chuckles came from a friend's one line commentary, used as the title to this post. Here "stupid" means "take too many risks". It's part of our evolutionary -biology and -psychology as a species, that male stupidity, that over-willing-ness to take a risk for sex. Women's economic sexual investment is staggering and immediately physical: their bodies change. For life. Become pregnant once and the "fix is in" as they say.

And we're not even getting into the financial, social, cultural, etc., challenges and changes that occur.

Now for Men

Male directed financial, social, and cultural changes occurring due to pregnancy are relatively recent in human history, specifically western cultural history and really only go back a few hundred years or so. These changes are pretty much due to post-Protestantism and the burgeoning concept of social responsibility. When someone tells a male to "take responsibility for your actions" that request is bucking several million years of evolutionary biologic design, several thousand years of psycho-cultural training and acquisition, and so much sexual neuromorphology that one might as well tell the stars to stop shining.

So, due to these design, training, and morphologic tendencies, because the male's investment is far less psycho-physical than the female's, men will risk more — literally put more money, territory, blood, ... at risk — for sex than women will. Generally speaking.

Ever seen a guy hot-dogging on the slopes or waves or streets while checking out of the corner of his eye if the women are paying attention?

But Does It Work?

First answer — the fact that so many males are willing to pay for sex with risky behavior (putting a psycho- and neuro-economics slant on it) is an indication that the reward has been there often enough for evolutionary biasing to provide males sufficient neurophysiology to engage in such behavior.

That's a neuroscientist's way of saying "Yes, it works."

Does it work all the time?

Easy answer — No! (thank goodness).

Recognize that not all risks are physical. Some are psychological, some are emotional, some are spiritual. The type of risk a male is willing to undertake is indicative of what the male values and what he's willing to advertise as "I'll put this at risk for you" (again, psycho- and neuro-economics kicks in). Sexual advertising is also part of our evolutionary history and is the basis of mate-selection. The peacock's beautiful plumage, the lion's wonderful mane, the web-entrepreneur's Testarossa — wait a second. That can't be right. I'm driving a ten-year-old Jeep Cherokee. Maybe I'm advertising differently? — are all signals of health and progenic capability, things females of all species look for during mate selection.

And the type of advertising is an indication of the type of audience desired.

Males — even those in healthy, happy, monogamous relationships — will put something at risk as a demonstration of their progenic worth to their desired companion.

This is where behavioral ethology and more come into play. There are certain female psychologies and ages where physically risky behavior serves as a sexual stimulant. However, at a certain point females mature and, seeing physically risky behavior, think "That guy's not a good prospect. He's dangerous to himself and might not be around to help me raise the kids/have a good life/pay off the mortgage/...".

However, the male who counsels with his significant other or desired significant other before taking on financial, professional, psychological, ... risky behavior?

Ah...well...that male has demonstrated a willingness to partner, to place the significant other on an equal setting, perhaps even at times a higher, counselor, setting.

So gentlemen, evaluate what you're putting at risk in light of your partner's possible responses. You'll get sex and much, much more.

Where "Happy Valentine's Day!" meets "Love doesn't come with a pricetag!"

Ah, Valentine's Day.

Romantic to everyone except the wonderful women I had the pleasure of lunching with late last week. A good size group of them, ages from late thirties to middle fifties, all either business owners or executives in business, mixed ethnic backgrounds although predominantly white.

And to a T they all Scrooged Valentine's Day with a resounding "Bah, humbug!"

The rallying cry could be summed up in a single thought, "If my partner needs a special day to show me I'm loved, that love doesn't mean much."

Flowers, champagne, cards, candy, jewelry, definitely negligees and things even more explicit were universally denounced.

High on the list of "that's good" was impromptu time together. "My husband sometimes comes running up to me and kisses me, then runs back to finish what he's doing. I love that." Cuddling under a blanket on a chilly winter's night watching a favorite show or movie was up there. A quiet dinner with mobiles off where they talked scored lots of points. "One thing I really hate is his damn iPhone. I want to grab it out of his hands and say 'You're talking to me. Let's finish our conversation first'."

I questioned that. Each person in the room had some kind of mobile device and a good number had more than one. Does technology get in the way of relationship?

"It can but only if you let it."

Preventing that takes two partners, doesn't it?

That was the slippery slope. The women in this group didn't want peaks of attention on special days so much as equal amounts of attention on all days with reasonable peaks and troughs as life allows.

So, guys, send a card or flowers or candy or jewelry if you must, but put down your phone first. Send the kids out to a movie for the evening. Surprise her with an evening of genuine sincerity and appreciation for her as your partner in life.

She is, after all, much more than your "wife".

I'm Nine Feet Tall and Six Feet Wide

I know this will come as a shock to many readers and I apologize ahead of time for bursting anyone's bubble.

It seems that men exaggerate certain aspects of themselves when it comes to getting dates.

I know. Shocking and true.

I recently took part in a discussion about social stereotypes, stigma and stereotype threat, things made popular in *Whistling Vivaldi: And Other Clues to How Stereotypes Affect Us* (Issues of Our Time) by Claude M. Steele. Most of the discussion was well reasoned and...sane. It got a little crazy when the subject turned to what the genders expect from each other when it comes to dating.

Women, it seems, learn very early on (guesses went down to 13 years old, consensus was 14.5 years old) that guys will...exaggerate...about anything and everything. Working males will put themselves at risk to demonstrate success. Some will buy large, flashy vehicles that they can't afford, for example.

I wondered if this accounted for Ford truck sales. Pickups, muscle cars, roadsters. Older males, it seems, favor vehicles that indicate skill and knowledge rather than raw power.

I once commented that the size of the tires on such vehicles was inversely proportional to the size of a man's...

Anyway, a woman I knew told me that wasn't necessarily true.

All males will buy large, expensive watches, jewelry — anybody remember the "Italian Horns"? That's what we called them. Evidently you can still buy them. How many of you knew that the number of curves had meaning? Imposed by the women. And evidently accurate.

And guys, it's not what you think.

Some men, if they can't get the upper body profile they believe women crave via the gym or heredity, will resort to cosmetic surgery or other means.

I was reminded of studies conducted with male bower birds. Male bower birds arrange their nesting areas to make themselves appear larger to prospective mates.

I was impressed at the renditions of male vanity.

And that it crossed species so easily.

And then I asked, "Isn't what you're describing the male version of the woman who gets cosmetic enhancements? Not just surgery to promote health, but surgery to enhance secondary sexual characteristics with the goal of stimulating mate-seeking behavior in desirable males? ..."

No, really. I said it just like that, I swear.

"... Or who purchase enhancing or somewhat revealing clothing?"

Okay, that I did say pretty much like that. And that's when things really opened up.

Men, it seems, don't look beyond the covers. The majority of men, anyway (I was graciously informed I was an exception. I don't really think I am, and I wasn't going to argue the point). Women know when men are posturing and won't be able to live up to the promise.

"And men don't, you think?"

Men do. They just don't care.

And so the discussion went until we agreed that in all such cases the core belief of the individual was one of lack, of not being enough in and of themselves, of simply not being comfortable being who they are.

That caused many of the females in the discussion to emit a quiet, glassy eyed, deep throated moan of desire. "Finding a man comfortable with himself. Yeah."

It was acknowledged that women, like men, look at arm-candy first.

Sad, true, and at least admitted to among this group of social academics.

But then it got into "who's for this night" versus "who's for always" and there was general agreement that the person picked first often isn't the person who lasts.

Long term, successful relationships, it is agreed, are based on what's within.

So to both sexes, some advice that reminds me of the old adage regarding buying stereo equipment, "Figure out what you can afford and spend half of that on speakers."

Guys and gals, you can purchase and enhance if you want, but spend half of that enhancing budget on what's inside you.

It pays off again and again and again.

Cruzin' and Male Social Networks

When I was a teenager (long ago, in the before time), Denny, Jack, George and sometimes Don (if his parents let him out) would get in my '64 Mercury Comet and drive up and down Elm Street cruzin' for chicks.

I have no idea what we would have done if we actually encountered girls willing to get in the car with us. We were, as most were, all bluster and little else. Jack was our designated "man of the world" but I think that was because his parents were divorced — an oddity back then — so *de facto* he knew more about how the world worked than we did.

No, there's no logic in that. You did see the word "teenager" in the above, correct?

Anyway, we were *Cruzin'*. I believe it was a long-standing tradition among males in my era and something given heraldic meaning in *American Graffiti*.

I assume that Cruzin' still occurs. In a sense it has to. It's based on human biology and evolution, and my description above gives away a significant clue to its purpose: it's a mating behavior.

Cruzin' takes the form of male groups going out to bars together, to sporting and entertainment venues, a group of guys going on spring break together to some exotic locale, ...

The consistent element is that a group — a social network — of unattached males are together publicly. It's mating behavior because it's easier for males to find mates when the males are in groups than when they're solo.

You're Kidding, Right?

Males in groups are more likely to find individual mates because the females get to evaluate the male against other males immediately. Single males on the prowl allow females to think "Hmm...maybe I'll wait for the next one" while males together allow females to do immediate comparison shopping (so to speak), something like "Hmm...better eyes than bachelor #1, cuter smile than bachelor #2, nicer hands than bachelor #3, ..." Anybody remember *The Dating Game*, the forerunner of today's *Tinder*, *Bumble*, *OkCupid* and associated dating apps?

Males Cruzin' with a social network actually benefits individual males' mating potentials. Studies demonstrated that non-social grouped "attractive" males engage in long term conversations with potential partners less often than social grouped "average" males. Ditto leaving coupling venues ("bars") coupled rather than singled.

Not to mention that, much like any other competitive sport, having your buddies right there with you means you'll have some encouragement to talk to that little cutie at the end of the bar and some cover when some other male social group member goes territorial, right (aka the bar scene in *Good Will Hunting*)?

So guys, cruze.

Ladies, much as I mentioned before when quoting a friend's great aunt, feel free to swim, just don't go in the water.

Guys! Lower Your Voice!

Guys, want to be noticed more often when you're out and about?

Easy. Lower your voice.

No, I don't mean talk quietly, I mean literally lower the pitch of your voice.

A study of college and university women conducted in southern England, the US, Canada, and Brazil had women listen to a conversation among two males (A and B). They couldn't see the two males, they could only hear them. The conversation - about their workday - was scripted and recorded so that all female participants heard the same conversation. The only variant was that the conversation was recorded twice. In version one the male with the mid-baritone voice read part A and the male with the tenor voice read part B, in version two the males switched the parts they read.

And it didn't matter who said what, well over 75% of the women participating found the mid-baritone male more interesting and worth meeting.

How low can you go?

It seems the baritone speaking range is optimal when mate-seeking. When male voices were electronically modified so that the lower pitch was in the bass range, women's interest changed from wanting to meet to wanting to see who's voice it was, a shift from "that's interesting" to "what is that?"

What was also interesting was that language played a role. Brazilian females found low pitch, quiet voices more interesting, native English speakers were more intrigued when they knew exactly what was being said.

An Example and Taking It a Bit Further

My natural voice is quite low pitched. Susan (wife/partner/Princess) tells me I sound like I'm either purring or rumbling when I talk in my natural voice. I learned in my teens to modulate my pitch into a higher register to make it easier for people to understand the words I'm speaking. If I don't, whatever words I'm speaking get lost in the background.

An added bonus to modulating one's pitch is being able to convince people more easily of things they should or shouldn't do. Modulate your pitch to close to the other person's – good!

Modulate your voice to their speaking pitch – Fantastic!

The reason is simple and based on consciousness studies. Most people talk to themselves in their normal speaking voice, meaning they're used to hearing their own voice inside their head, whether they vocalize or not.

Match their speaking pitch and the brain immediately becomes attentive because – hey! – the person must be talking to themselves.

The intriguing part is this works for both sexes and with a slight caveat. No woman wants to hear her own voice coming from a male throat, ditto men hearing their own voice emitted from a female throat. In these cases, come an octave away and mimic speech tones, patterns, and language.

Works great.

Especially in crowds.

Like when you're addressing a group of the opposite sex and about to say something they don't want to hear.

Romance is Risky

Ever seen that great John Wayne-Maureen O'Hara movie, *The Quiet Man*? Remember the scene where they want to have some time alone together and steal a tandem bicycle to get away from everyone?

Watch the movie. They don't borrow and return, they take, steal. And they discard it without ever bringing it back.

How about the highly romanticized (and highly incorrect) modern Bonnie and Clyde myth?

Anybody care for a bit of Lancelot and Guinevere?

Or consider your own life. Have you ever been romantically involved with someone?

More importantly, did you survive?

I ask because studies the world over indicate people experiencing romantic love engage in riskier behavior than those not so involved. You can be in a loving, stable relationship and avoid risks. You can be uninvolved in any relationship and not looking for one and avoid risks.

But get that heart pounding and eyes fluttering and sweat glands pumping and love going and by golly, anything's fair game.

Okay, not quite anything

Romantic love provides humans with an interesting side effect. The brain and various glands are pumping out all sorts of chemicals to give you that "I'm in LOVE!!!" feeling.

A side effect is your executive functions (the most advanced part of the brain) take backseats now and again because the lower brain regions (the ones we share with all creatures great and small from reptiles on up) are coming on strong, front and center, because your body is preparing to...umm...get some.

And anybody who tells you your hormones are on overdrive when you're in romantic love is...either forgetful, delusional, or inexperienced themselves.

People in romantic love (and precisely because they're in romantic love) will take impromptu days off to go to the beach, go hiking, go anywhere and just to be around each other.

The other side effect of all this is the desire to look really, Really, REALLY appealing to your newfound partner (romantic, risk-taking love occurs most often with someone new, as in "love at first sight"). Strangely, the lower brain regions - those parts we share with all creatures from reptiles on up - don't think demonstrating a good job, a steady income, sound financial reasoning, economical spending habits, reasonable, comfortable clothing, et cetera, are really appealing.

Swim in freezing water, bath with sharks, sky-jump, rock-climb, buy an expensive car, buy designer-name clothes, take vacations to exotic locations without considering how one will pay for them, ... these are things the lower brain thinks are great ideas.

The Cure

Well, there really isn't one. Not yet.

But the higher brain does put the brakes on. It puts the brakes on by observing the risks versus the rewards. Some people consider themselves the reward. Others don't want to lose that romantic feeling. Both are, in essence, lower brain junkies. All those fairy tales about the damsel in distress who swoons into the arms of her hero-savior-knight? Read your history. Never happened.

Ever met someone who's on their third, fourth, fifth, sixth, or higher marriage? Talk with them, watch their behaviors, and most often you'll discover they don't like being in love, they like *falling* in love. They don't want a stable relationship, they want the romance, i.e., the risk, and they demonstrate that need by flitting from one romantic relationship to the next. Think Liz Taylor, Zsa Zsa Gabor, Mickey Rooney, Marilyn Monroe, ... and you see people with serious issues. Or brain damage.

But in your life, if you're in a romantic relationship, give yourself a chance to let the romantic elements sojourn into a romance. Risky behavior is exhilarating, yes (that's why it's called "risky" behavior) and living in risk tasks the system more than necessary and leads to all sorts of physical challenges down the road.

Enjoy being romantic and give yourself a chance for romance. Your heart will throb in an entirely different way, and it'll do it for as long as you and your partner last.

The Gullibility of Love

Quick quiz: who's more susceptible to a come-on, regardless if it's from an overweight salesman with mustard stains on his tie or a mall huckster or ...

Would it be the gent on the prowl, the gent between relationships or the fellow infatuated with some immediate *amore*?

It turns out that the fellow who's starting or rekindling a relationship is much more susceptible to cons, scams and being taken in general.

What's very odd is the gender difference. Women starting or rekindling a relationship will be more on guard in general and, once they've made the psychological commitment to the other person, less guarded with that other person. Their susceptibility to cons, scams, etc., is highest at the time of decision, normal at all other times.

Well, good so far; being open, available and vulnerable to that special someone is what being in love is all about, and being less open, less available and less vulnerable to others is what being careful is all about.

You have to wonder about that "highest vulnerability at the time of the decision," don't you? Makes me wonder if there's something in the female psyche that essentially says, "Shut down the ability to make good social decisions for this, okay?"

But men starting relationships tend to get on a euphoric high and stay there for a bit. That good feeling, much like the runner's high or gym high, acts like a low-level, completely natural endorphic anesthetic that lessens the fatigue after a good workout. It lifts their spirits and causes a sense of *bon ami* that opens them to bad social decisions, interactions and arrangements.

Right when they're getting involved with someone. Seems like evolution working in reverse for both genders, doesn't it?

Again, gender differences apply. Once the euphoria has faded and until they've made a psychological commitment to that other person, men tend to withhold more from that other, a kind of "keeping their options open" mindset, that more often than not can destroy a relationship rather than nurture one.

Sad, when you think of it; it's as if men and women have two different competing cycles when it comes to commitment. The male's starts strong then grows weak until that psychological decision of "this is the one" is made, and then it grows strong(er) again. The female's starts weak then grows strong until the "this is the one" decision is made, then continues to grow.

Oddly, it's not evolution working in reverse. It's good evolutionary design, yet another holdover from our primitive ancestors that the primitive parts of our brains haven't shaken yet. The drive for species survival wins over good mate choice when no good mate choice presents itself.

So be careful out there. Especially if you've just fallen in love.

Women, Want to Be Ignored On Your Next Night Out?

Remember the internet brouhaha about a dress that was either blue and black or gold and white depending on who looked at it?

Good, because this post has nothing to do with that...kind of.

That dress looked different to different people based on several factors, some of which were the angle at which you looked at the dress, the lighting, so on and so forth.

It turns out that what people - specifically men - see when they look at clothing has lots to do with whether or not they'll attempt to chat you up. You can wear the most form fitting, body accentuating clothing and if that clothing is also brightly colored then men are less likely to be interested. I'm sure you'll be noticed, you just won't be hit on.

Here's another tidbit that can be useful. You're less likely to be chatted up if your clothing is all the same color, say a single color suit or color matched outfit. But wear color coordinated dress and blouse, pants and shirt, blah blah blah and stares of interest will turn into flirtatious chatter. Different colors allow the eye-brain to break up the image more easily and appreciate subtleties of shape and form that a single color outfit masks and hides.

So remember, if you want a quiet night out and not be bothered by anybody, wear something that's got a single, flamboyant color.

But if you want someone to approach, break things up a bit colorwise.

You never tell me you love me

One of the most frustrating arguments to watch goes something like this:

"You never tell me you love me."
"Of course I love you. Everybody knows I love you. I talk about you all the time."
"But you never *tell me* that you love me."

That middle line, the "Of course I love you. ..."? That'll be spoken by a male. It won't matter if this is a gay or straight relationship because males, as a group, aren't good at verbal communications.

And when those verbal communications are about feelings and emotions, i.e., about making oneself vulnerable?

Oy!

What's fascinating about this is that the male's last sentence, "I talk about you all the time.", is probably quite true. Men, as a group, will share information with other male or mixed gender peer groups gladly.

Note the use of "groups" in the above.

That's the kicker; men will talk up their partners in peer groups gladly, loudly, proudly and unequivocally. But one-on-one, in an intimate verbal moment? Not so much.

The disconnect here is that people like to hear that they're special, that they're loved, that someone special feels for them as they feel for that someone special.

Fortunately there are ways to reconnect. Does your significant other male lack verbal skills? Ask them to write you a love note. Nothing elaborate, just something for you to keep and hold to yourself. Most men are happy to do so. (Although sometimes trust can be an issue. Promise not to share it with anybody.) Their prose may be a little rough, a little awkward, and remember, it's a start.

Give them time. They'll be bringing you flowers, taking you out to dinner, the movies, and generally courting you all over again soon enough.

Appendix: Principles

What follows is a living document. Things are added. To date (45+ years), nothing's been deleted. Some comes from things my Grandfather taught me, some from life, some from my own studies, journeys, and what have you. A friend, learning much came from my Grandfather, nodded and congratulated me for keeping my Grandpa's teaching alive. "We've lost the elements of honoring the elders," she said.

Someone once asked me if I've lived up to the Principles myself.

"Hell no. That's why I write them down. So they can be a guide to me, so I'll know when I am not following them."

Like so much in my life, they are for me. If others benefit from them, wonderful (and it seems many do). But first and foremost, they are for me.

You may not like them all. You may only be comfortable with one or two.

Good start. Work to integrate them all. Find that difficult? As noted above, if they were easy for me to follow I wouldn't write them down.

I will offer you can't pick and choose. Or at least it seems most people can't. I haven't met anyone who's done so successfully, known many who have tried and failed.

One fellow studied them for a while and told me he couldn't find any contradictions in them. They seem internally consistent.

Reassuring, that.

"Does that mean you'll follow them?"

"No way. I've got a life to live."

And so it goes.

1. Do unto others as if they were you.

In other words, cut out the middle man. Treat others the way you treat yourself. People do this anyway. All we do is suggest you become aware of it.

2. Trust yourself.

Until you do this, you'll never be able to trust others and you'll put what trust you have in people who will hurt you.

3. Be Honest.

With yourself first because it makes it easier to be honest with others. Honesty will cost you and what it returns is worth it. Tell tall tales, lie with the best of them and exaggerate all you want when people know that's what you're doing. The rest of the time, be honest.

4. Respect people's boundaries and limits.

There's a difference between being selfish and being selfless. Realize what this means for you and you'll realize what it means for others.

5. Keep it Simple.

Because it's so much easier that way.

6. Take responsibility for your actions.

When you make a mistake and before anybody else knows the mistake has been made, raise your hand and say loud enough for others to hear you, "That one's mine. I did that." If the people around you are more interested in pointing their fingers at you and distancing themselves from you than helping you clean things up, you're standing around the wrong people. Let them distance themselves. They won't be around you when you succeed, and you will, because you'll have learned how to stand up tall, proud and free by recognizing, owning up to and cleaning up your own mistakes. From this you'll also learn compassion and dignity and how to help others clean up their mistakes, as well. Along with this ...

7. Mistakes are just that; You can reach again.

So learn to stretch when you have to and to recognize when what you're reaching for isn't something you'd want to hold in your hands. You'll be better for it and so will those who love you.

8. Innocence is not Naivety and vice-versa.

Think of this as a self-recognition of " ... wise as serpents and harmless as doves."

9. Your rights end where your willingness to harm and hurt begin.

If you need this one explained or you needed a moment to put this into a context you could get comfortable with, you are either intentionally ignorant (never a good plan) or hoping to excuse yourself for your.behavior towards others (also not a good plan)

10. Language is a tool, like Maslow's Hammer.

Some people think everything's a nail. Be neither. This is part 1.

11. Language is a tool, and can be Eliadeian.

Some people are or can become 2nd order thinkers. Be both. This is part 2.

12. Faith is with the heart, but the confession of faith is with the lips.

So until you can say it to at least two others, it ain't true and you and others will know it.

13. Everything is that simple.

As soon as you begin saying things are not quite that simple or that things aren't that easy, you've demonstrated you don't understand the true nature of the problem.

14. Be wary of those who only tell you of their successes.

They do not have a full view of life.

15. It is not easier to get forgiveness than permission.

Attempting to do so demonstrates a lack of concern and consideration for others.

16. Be thee not a respecter of men (or women).

Respect is earned through actions that are closely aligned with words, and both are externalizations of thoughts, beliefs and ideas, which brings us back to what you get when you squeeze an orange.

17. Do not go where you are not invited.

This, in all things, because being unwelcome can be a painful experience in more ways than one, and the corollary is that you'll always find your way to where you're wanted and loved.

18. Do not do what you are not asked to do.

Because until you are asked, you're doing it for yourself, not for them, and it may not be what they wanted in the first place.

19. People who don't ask for what they want deserve what they get.

So go ahead and ask. All a "no" means is that there must be other avenues you haven't explored yet.

20. Never, via your direct action or intentional inaction, allow others to come to harm.

And the minute you begin debating what "harm" is, you've already allowed it to happen.

21. If someone is drowning don't ask them "How wet is the water?"

Make sure your questions are relevant to the situation you are asking about. Think before you speak, otherwise be prepared for those around you to care more about keeping themselves dry than helping you to safety.

22. You are not your brother's (or your sister's) keeper.

Show people enough respect to let them make their own mistakes. That way they'll be able to appreciate their own successes.

23. If you can't think outside the box then you'll spend your life as someone else's package.

And maybe you're comfortable with that. We're not.

24. Don't feed someone when you're hungry.

You'll be jealous of what they eat and there's no guarantee there'll be any left for you when they're done.

25. In the Game of Life, let the other person win once in a while.

You'll learn to be humble, they'll learn to be gracious. At some point in time they'll figure out what you did, then they'll learn to be humble and you'll learn to be gracious.

26. What is a Dark Mystery to you is Perfectly Obvious to someone else (and vice versa).

So when you explain something to somebody, explain the obvious. When you leave something out and they don't get it, you're the fool, not them.

27. Everybody knows there are classes in society, any society.

Wise people don't speak of it. The wisest people don't show it.

28. Respect people who know the name of their waiter or waitress.

It shows they value people.

29. Everything is possible.

When you decide something is impossible all you've done is demonstrate the limitations of your resources.

30. To each of us is given a measure, to some great and to some so small as not to be noticed in the light of day.

How can we know that the greatest measure, without the efforts of those barely noticed as foundation or support or crown, will be enough? Therefore never slight nor be jealous of those whose measure is greater or less than yours, because to each of us is given a measure. It's not the measure that makes us great, it's what we do with our measure that gives us greatness.

31. You don't always need a reason to get something done.

Sometimes things just have to be done, and that is reason enough.

32. Own your history. Don't be owned by it.

You are the only one who has the power to change the universe you live in.

33. Sometimes you just have to let the fool be slapped.

People know when they're not being upfront, honest, above board, ... , and nine times out of ten they want to be caught because it gives shape, form, and substance to the world around them. You honor them and yourself by catching them. Regarding that one out of ten that doesn't want to be caught? Put up walls between yourself and them. They will be a danger to both themselves and to you.

34. Never be afraid to appear a fool when asking a question.

It's the ones who won't ask questions who are truly the fools.

35. Be wary of people who enjoy casting large shadows.

It is better to be the light that allows shadows to exist, that lights the way for others, than to be in someone else's darkness.

36. Courage is not the absence of fear. Courage is what you do when you're afraid.

Be Courageous. It will cost you relationships, no doubt, but you'll be able to sleep at night.

37. When someone is hanging onto a cliff by their fingernails, don't ask them if they want to play catch.

Another example of making sure your questions are relevant to the situation. People in need, people under stress and strain, when distracted, suffer. Make sure you help rather than hurt.

38. Let your dreams create your capabilities.

Never believe that what you are now is all you ever shall be.

39. Some will ask, "What do you want?" Others with, "Who are you?" To answer either, you must first answer "Am I who I want to be?"

Whether known or not, spoken or not, it is the first question that must be answered.

40. Laws are the boundaries societies place upon the spirit.

Be boundless. You may be in a society of one, but being alone is often the price of freedom.

41. Never allow yourself to be blinded by those who lack vision.

Surround yourself with those who encourage you to see, even if they can not. It is much to be preferred than to be around those who won't allow you to see because they themselves can not.

42. Shame is a gift given by someone who fears you.

This can be a hard lesson to learn. The only reason for someone to make you feel ashamed is to control you, and love has no need for control.

43. If you follow your path long enough, eventually you'll discover your dreams.

Therefore it is up to you to make sure your dreams are something you want to discover.

44. and in keeping with the above, Paths reveal themselves to you if you let them.

They are not always straight and often not obvious, therefore it's up to you to follow or not as you decide.

45. Acceptance is not Understanding.

Keep separate the things you accept and the things you understand. A few items will be in both camps, a lot of items won't. Knowing the difference means knowing what you're willing to change versus what you're willing to let change you, and the world of difference is there.

46. As with most things, if you're willing to go just a little bit further than you've ever gone before, an entirely new world is opened onto you.

Explore to the limits of your abilities and willingness. It's the only way to know how big you really are.

47. Is it better to see the end, to hear its answer when you call its name, or to be there?

Answer these and you'll know what eternity means to you.

48. True Authority becomes such by acknowledging, understanding and incorporating all points of view, especially those that disagree.

Authority can not exist without growth and change, and authority that can't include or disprove disagreement is no authority at all.

49. Success is not synonymous with Achievement.

People can have successful careers and have achieved nothing in their life, while people who've achieved but one thing are successful beyond measure. Success means you've grown (no small achievement, that). Achievement means you've helped someone else grow (and to be willing just to take on that task indicates you're a success).

50. "Chaos, once defined, can be the most organized system there is." and "Don't burn your bridges before they hatch." are two orthogonal statements and their intersection is you.

Take the time to realize that these two statements are equations of existence and that they define a universe of possibilities. Recognize that if they intersect you are the intersection and that if they don't intersect you're denying yourself a universe of possibilities.

51. Always be willing to share your story and always be respectful of the stories of others.

Tell people "I will tell you as much of my story as you wish to know, but I will never share your story with others nor will I share another's story with you." Understand this and you'll understand your own and other's boundaries, where you begin and end and how your words can heal and hurt others.

52. If you can't clearly say "No" then nobody will know when you're saying "Yes".

So be clear and concise in all your communications when a "No" or a "Yes" will do. People will appreciate it and confusions will quickly melt away.

53. Handing over control is not giving up responsibility.

Hand over control of something to someone else and they become your responsibility as well as whatever you have control of. Consider this an opportunity to teach, yourself and them.

54. Never let your limitations be someone else's limitations.

You've probably worked long and hard to get the ones you have. Don't share them. Similarly, honor the ones others have that you don't. They worked just as hard to get theirs as you did to get yours.

55. Sometimes the best lesson is recognizing that someone is not your teacher.

It can save both of you a lot of pain and sorrow.

56. Paddle Plato's Life Boat with Ockham's Razor.

Find a theoretical structure that supports all data, even conflicting data, and find a theoretical structure that supports it all without resorting to unnecessary entities. This is where The Principle of Rich Observation meets The Principle of Parsimony. Live there. Be there. Be it.

57. You must be dancing yourself if you want to dance with somebody.

You can not find what you're looking for until and unless you're willing to first be it yourself.

58. Eliminate Variables, Remove Ambiguities.

You are going to make mistakes in life (see Principles 6, 7, and 22). It's possible to minimize those mistakes by eliminating as many unknowns as possible from the situation before you act. You can further minimize mistakes by removing all ambiguous information before you act. It isn't possible to ignore ambiguous information and it's usually possible to act in a way that doesn't require making use of the ambiguous data. Be patient. Ambiguous situations tend to resolve themselves given enough time. How do they resolve? By eliminating unknowns.

59. Be An Enemy of the People, point out the naked Emperor, protect The Old Man and tell people about The Rock.

You may be the only one who knows the truth and in truth, you're the only one who can know your own truth. However, that doesn't make the truth incorrect and your sharing it can possibly save lives. Even if it costs you yours.

60. It is perfectly useless to know the answer to the wrong question.

So before you answer another's question ask yourself if the question is worth answering at all.

61. Never cure a singer of their voice.

Sometimes people's gifts can frighten or disturb us, hence their gifts go unappreciated. Take a moment to make sure your goal is to be just and that your pursuit isn't just for yourself at the expense of others.

62. Choice is better than no choice.

This isn't Free Will versus Predestination, this is right here, right now, do you want to be in control of your life or give up control? The latter leads to victimization and can't be healthy for anyone involved. The former leads to opportunity and possible sacrifice, but it'll be your choice to sacrifice if you do.

63. Don't label people (for both your sakes).

It's sometimes helpful to assign labels to people so long as you remember that people are not objects, labels are like boxes and boxes can become coffins. For both of you.

64. Work honestly, accurately, and unbiasedly.

Doing so will be your testimony. And while some may despise you, the majority will recognize that you honor them through your work and return that honor a hundred-fold.

65. A worker is worthy of their wages.

Recognize that nothing is free. That's first. Somebody is paying some where at some time any time some thing is done. Directly paying the worker for work done demonstrates you value them and their work, that you recognize them as equals in a fair-exchange, and (perhaps most importantly) that you respect yourself enough to know your own value is not in question. That last one throw you? Then go elsewhere. The only time people want something for free is when they're not sure of the value of their own efforts because the price people are willing to pay is a measure of the value they place on their request. Want something for free? Then it has little value to you. Willing to pay? Then it's important to you. It's as simple as that.

The other side of this is that the worker can ask for wages in other than coin of the realm (and barter doesn't count. Barter is mutually agreed to coin of the realm). Recognize that the only commerce besides coin of the realm is with a piece of yourself — your time, your strength, your thoughts, your word, your knowledge, your wisdom, your friendship, your oath. Be careful with these. Coin is far cheaper than heart.

66. Act with kindness even though you don't know the outcome.

Never doubt that something you said or didn't say, did or didn't do, etc., changed the universe in some incredible way. The Universe's concept of the Butterfly Effect is "You said hello to someone walking down the street whom you didn't know therefore a lifeless planet is starting to form oceans."

67. Until you've gathered all the data available and understood its significance in the situation under study, your decisions regarding the situation are inherently flawed.

Even if they're the correct decisions, the decision process is flawed and outcomes are reproducible due more to luck than knowledge because you never know if the lacking data is contributing 1 or 99% to a complete solution. Explaining observed outcomes without complete knowledge of what's causing them is a fool's goal.

68. Forgive others so that you can be released from their grasp.

Forgiveness isn't done for others, it's done for yourself, to help you let go of the emotions that bind you to someone who wronged you. This does not mean you must love them, only that you may let them go.

69. Faith, until it is tested, is just an opinion.

It doesn't matter if faith takes the form of fealty to a friend, a place, a country, a product, an idea, a life-partner or a deity, until that faith is tested it is just opinion about your relationship to a friend, a place, et cetera. Tested, you know the limits of your faith and limits are just that, neither failure nor triumph, only today's boundaries and limits, only how far you'll go today in this particular test.

70. Technology is not how we make and keep relationships. We make and keep relationships because of who we are, not what tools we use to stay in touch.

Everybody's lives are hectic. If you can't get everything done you want to do and are missing appointments/meetings/friends/what-have-you, getting more technology won't organize your day because time isn't your problem, you are. You have as much time in your day as Michelangelo, Galileo, Newton, Einstein, Gandhi, Mother Teresa, Buddha, Socrates, ...

71. An individual can only receive a certain benefit if others are willing to take on a certain burden.

Remember, the Universe works in balance. From Principles 1, 4, 6, 9, 20, ... , remember that what you take you owe. Think you don't often enough, think this doesn't apply to you often enough and you'll find yourself on the long end of burden. Not a happy place.

72. When someone shares their success with you, focus on them, not you. There's no need to compare their success to yours. This is their moment, not yours.

Imagine your toddler or a friend's toddler taking their first step. Would you tell them about your first step? This Principle is a corollary to 14. Help people celebrate their successes. Especially those they struggled for. And earned.

73. Only teach those willing to be taught.

People demonstrate a real learning desire by how they ask and what they do with what you give them. Don't teach because you believe you have something to share. You may not teach what they want to learn, they may not want to learn what you want to teach.

Real teaching is about helping people discover their own way, their own doors, their own understanding. We teach best by our actions. Be careful with yours.

74. Any step is a step in the right direction when you're lost.

Imagine you're lost, not sure where you are but sure you're not where you want to be. All that matters is you move. Right then, right there, direction is irrelevant. Pick any direction and take one small step. Now evaluate: Are things better or not. No? Take one small step in another direction, doesn't matter which. Yes? Take another small step in the same direction and evaluate again.

When you don't know what you're doing or where you are, the important thing is to do something. Standing around waiting to be rescued keeps you lost and a victim of your own unsurety. Do something and you're less lost because you learn where you should be heading and you're sure where you shouldn't be heading.

Appendix: Definitions

What Was NextStage?

Long, long ago and in an internet far, far away, there was a little, tiny company with a base, disruptive technology that planted itself in twenty different fields (industries). That little, tiny company took root in nineteen of the twenty.

Not bad for a freakin' farmboy from Nova Scotia, right?

Okay, now seriously ...

From 1995 to 2016 Susan (wife/partner/Princess) and I had a company called *NextStage Evolution* based on a technology I created in our basement (I know it sounds apocryphal and it's true. You can read about it in *Reading Virtual Minds Volume I: Science and History* http://nlb.pub/MindsV1). According to the USPTO (United States Patent and Trade Office - the place you get patents in the US, and these are their words, not ours) "NextStage has created a technology that allows any machine to understand and respond to human thought through any human-machine interface."

Such a technology (in the mid-late 1990s) was *base* - meaning, as one of our early investors said - it was like plastic. We could make a milk bottle out of it, a car dashboard, picnic cutlery, basketballs, anything. It was disruptive because it could change how lots of things were done.

That it did, in many industries and not all.

Eventually the technology - which we called *Evolution Technology* - was in use in some 125 countries. We had offices in four countries and representation in about thirty others.

We could have been even more widespread, and our Principles (in Appendix: Principles) stopped us.

Read through those Principles and you learn a lot about us, the people we hired, the companies we worked with, and what we were willing to do.

And after some twenty years, we needed a break. We started off-loading pieces of *Evolution Technology* to the companies and people we thought would use it wisely and well.

So far, so good.

Shortly after this off-loading process began, Susan said, "I've never seen you happier than when you're writing your stories. We don't have to worry about money anymore, so I want you to write your stories from now on."

Ever obedient, I did and am.

By the way, that "freakin' farmboy from Nova Scotia" line comes from my demonstrating *Evolution Technology* to the then Dean of MIT's Sloan School. At the end of the demonstration, he rolled his eyes and muttered (in front of our then VP), "I have the whole goddamn Media Center down the street from me and some f'ing farmboy from Nova Scotia figures this out?"

I stared at him for a moment and he met my gaze.

"I said that out loud, didn't I?"

"Yep."

Define NextStageologist

I mentioned in *Define NextStage* about people we hired. We hired from all over the globe, all races, all ethnic groups, all genders, all nationalities. There were three things all of them had in common:

1. An unsatiable curiosity
2. Colloquial fluency in two or more languages
3. Lots of life experience (they could be chronologically young so long as they had lots of life experience)

We knew going in we were going to be a different company. All our people were work-on-demand, not employees per se, and we paid them well enough they could afford private insurance, vacations, holidays, and the like. We had a firm three-strikes policy; you could make any one type of mistake twice. A third time with the same kind of mistake and you were out (because you weren't learning). But you could make lots of different kinds of mistakes so long as you learned and grew from them.

We also paid for them to go to school and take any classes they wished, no obligation for repayment and no grade requirements (that's the unsatiable curiosity department). We figured anything you learned would benefit both you and us, even if what you learned was the class or training was worthless to you.

The language fluency requirement dealt with *Evolution Technology* being partially based on language (my patents covered anthropology, linguistics, mathematics, neuroscience, and a bunch of other disciplines. One of our people once counted and came up with 120. Nice grouping, that, and mainly because I borrowed from lots of disciplines rather than reinvent what I needed when someone else already did it. This is called translational research, and is mentioned in some of this book's chapters).

Also regarding language and life experience, we wanted people who knew language is a tool, i.e., if someone's language or what they say upsets you, first recognize what they say has more to do with them than you, and second use your upsetness as a tool to learn more about your own issues rather than being hostile to them and theirs.

And there's probably more.

We're still in touch with many of them, and all were and are our teachers.

Who are yours?

And What Was The NextStage Irregular?

NextStage had clients all over the world, and many of them were researchers themselves (Susan and I come from heavy research backgrounds). Business clients constantly asked if we could get *Evolution Technology* to do certain things and, if the problem intrigued me, Susan et al had a tough time holding me back from solving it. Most times it only involved defining the root elements of the problem, writing the mathematics involved in the root definitions, then teaching *ET* (that's what we ended up calling *Evolution Technology*) to do the math.

And each time we came up with interesting research or needed people to test a tool developed to solve a client problem, we let people know via our newsletter, *The NextStage Irregular*, so called because we were NextStage and we never sent it out at regular intervals.

Hey, it was our sandbox, we could play in it the way we liked.

Tales Told 'Round Celestial Campfires

Volume 2

Please enjoy three stories from Joseph's upcoming book, available winter 2025.

Don Quitamo Sails

Don Quitamo rested his head on fine silk pillows and pulled the most excellent satin sheets over his body. Waves rocked his ship lulling him to sleep.

"Sleep well, Lord Quitamo."

His cabin door closed quietly and latched, secured. He relaxed and allowed his mind to wander. Seldom did The Lady Eglesia's captain get a full night's rest.

Behind closed lids the cabin grew dim. He thought 'She snuffed out the candles' and soon slept.

How long he slept he wasn't sure. The ship chronometer's eyes glowed in the dark, moving back and forth as they ticked off the seconds of the watch, its tail swishing rhythmically as if time, too, obeyed the sea's waves.

First Mate León, his shoulders like a lion's and his hair a golden halo about his head, called through the horn. "Your forgiveness, Lord Quitamo. The Merchant Vessel Tyree hails us from the shoulders of Orion."

He shrugged off sleep with his satin sheets, rose and reached for his cutlass in one continuous motion. "I know no Merchant Vessel Tyree. What colors do they hail?"

"They hail safe and well, Lord Quitamo. They say they've been followed through four starfields but the other ship won't identify."

"Call for full sail."

His command spread like fire. The Lady Eglesia spread her wings until so much white filled the sky nebulae darkened beneath them.

The Lady Eglesia, the smartest ship of the fleet, emboldened her icon and stood it before him. "Where are we questing today, Lord Quitamo?"

"Show me suns I've never seen. Show me skies that have never known man."

The Lady Eglesia's ports opened. Energies spread along her sides like water spilling from a deck's good washing. In a moment her hull hardened such that no life, no forces, weapons neither energy nor mass driven, could penetrate her.

"Now, my lord?"

"Now."

Once again her wings lifted, filling with so much sunlight she rose from the oceans and gravity no longer claimed her.

"Prepare me for the bowsprit."

He strode confidently, knowing The Lady Eglesia would protect her Good Captain, and in a moment felt her energies caress and cover him with a second flesh. Seals opened and closed as he walked until he stood with nothing but space beneath his feet.

The Lady Eglesia sent her energies forward, questing like dolphins in the night, leaping above the surface of the space-time continuum until they found entry, and diving they pulled her through the folds of space to the Tyree, her aft guns blazing at a ship flying no colors, dark in the night, the Tyree's shells falling far from their mark.

The Lady Eglesia surfaced from deep space, Lord Quitamo's Golden Sunfish on her prow.

The Tyree's mainlight signaled: May the Tides of Space befriend thee, Lord Quitamo.

Don Quitamo gave the order and The Lady Eglesia's lights signaled back: And you as well, Good Captain.

Quitamo called into the horn, "Bring me along side her."

First Lieutenant Oso, The Lady Eglesia's gunnery officer, called back. "The far ship won't answer a hail, Good Captain, and her battledoors are open. She could be preparing to fire."

"Lady Eglesia, rig for battle. Prepare the batteries. Strengthen your hull and sides."

Massive cannon rose from their berths, gained their stations at port, aft, starboard, and bow doors. Her sails hardened and grew transparent. Cables of unpenetrable steel shot through her decks, wrapped her hull and keel, fortified her masts. "I sail at your service, My Captain."

"Bring us alongside. Make us a barrier between the Tyree and whoever challenges her."

León kept a steady eye on the two ships they neared. "We know not the Merchant Vessel Tyree, My Captain. This could be a trap. We'd be caught between two enemy ships."

Lord Don Quitamo smiled a knowing smile. "And if we don't act to protect the Queen's ships? Any who know us would know the game is up and fire as soon as our hesitation showed. Bring us alongside, I say! Bring us alongside."

"Aye, Captain"'s echoed up and down the deck, from top to bottom deck, into the hold dark as night and up to the Crow's Nest, even now dipping towards the ocean's swells, the yardarm already whitecapping water.

"Mount the iron topsail. Bring me more speed."

The Tyree's captain, Gabrious by name, called across space's briny depths. "They are pirates, Lord Quitamo."

The Lady Eglesia came alongside, her mighty energies extending her hull to protect the Tyree's crew.

"Bring forth our guns. Let them stand fast, not run, until we trade with them."

The far ship stopped in the night. "They are hailing, Lord Quitamo."

"Show them our colors."

Tyree's captain called forth, "What manner of craft is she? I've not seen her like before."

Don Quitamo pulled forth his spyglass and lifted it to his eye. "She is a mothership."

"I've not heard of such a vessel."

"An Old Earth term. Misused from its original intention. There are not many like her. She is a mother formed as a ship. She gives birth to whatever the need."

Mono called from the Lookout, "She's flying pirate colors, Captain."

Lord Quitamo smiled up into the rigging as Mono clambered down. "Thank you. You have keen eyes for one of your kind."

"I sail at my Captain's pleasure, Lord Quitamo."

Gabrious pondered. "Old Earth? You know of Old Earth? Have you been there? They say there are treasures beyond thought waiting..."

"No. Once, perhaps. Not now. The Aegons took all that remained long ago, before the skies became seas."

Gabrious looked back at the far ship. "What could pirates want with such a ship?"

Don Quitamo unsheathed his cutlass and sliced the Merchant Vessel Tyree's Captain Gabrious from stem to stern. "To birth a one such as you, foul thing."

Gabrious fell apart, his gutted feathers scattering in the interstellar winds. "I should have known. Only the captain of a four poster could have guessed."

Don Quitamo took his pistoler from his belt and shot Gabrious dead.

A voice summoned Lord Quitamo from his deed. "Donald? Donald Quitamo, are you asleep? Do I have to come in there?"

Lord Quitamo rallied Mono and Oso and León. "Come, my fine crew, we must flee to the holds!"

"Donald Quitamo, I told you to put those pirate and science fiction picture books down. You can take your stuffed animals to bed with you but that's all. Now turn off your lights and go to sleep."

Footsteps asail The Lady Eglesia's outer hull, sudden and troubling.

Mono's eyes go from mate to mate to Captain and back. "I think she means to board us."

Covers are yanked from off their heads. Feathers from Don Quitamo's pillow flutter into the air and slowly descend.

Lord Quitamo looks up and smiles a fierce grin, facing his invader boldly. "We killed the Aegon imposter, Mom."

"Donald Quitamo, give me that flashlight. Why your father buys you these books and reads you these stories I don't know. Now put those books away, young man."

Don Quitamo stares back, defiant, feathers settling on his head and face. He puffs one away from his mouth.

His challenge is met with a kiss on the brow and a tuck of the blanket.

A massive shadow fills the cabin. A deep voice chuckles. "Which one is it, Donny?"

"We killed the Aegon imposter, Dad."

The deep voice of the intergalactic overlord speaks in Don Quitamo's defense. "He killed the Aegon imposter, Sylvie."

"Oh, you two!"

She takes Donald's flashlight and shines it on his cat-face clock. "Do you see that? When the big whisker is on 12 and the little whisker is on 8, that's it. Understand?"

Don Quitamo glances at the ship's chronometer, its eyes glowing in the dark, moving back and forth as its whiskers count off the minutes, its tail swishing with each second's passing.

Lord Quitamo nods his assent.

The intergalactic overlord's shadow fades, his voice carried from distant suns. "He killed the Aegon imposter, Sylvie."

"Shh!"

The door closes. The lights dim until only The Lady Eglesia's mainlight remains.

"There! Avast! Pirates off the main!"

Oso is back at his guns, Mono climbs the mast, León takes the helm, and all three cry out in victory, "Don Quitamo sails!"

The Magic Tassels

There was once a little boy who left his village and returned knowing how to journey the way shaman do. He returned to his people wearing tassels on his wrists and everybody who saw these tassels knew they were magic but nobody said anything to him about them.

Each day, the young boy helped tend the village herds and fields, each evening he ate with the old and not-so-old, the young and not-so-young in the village. He laughed at their jokes and made some of his own, cried at their grief and learned all of his own.

One evening, a little girl came to the boy. "Boy, what are those tassels you wear on your arms?"

She did this at the village fire. Everyone grew quiet to hear what the now older boy would answer.

He smiled at the little girl. "What do you see, little one?"

"I see snakes," she said. "Big, beautiful snakes. Snakes to ride on and carry me away."

The boy nodded. "Thank you, little girl. Thank you for telling me what these tassels on my arms are. Now I know they are snakes. Thank you very much."

The little girl smiled and laughed and the older boy did, too, as the little girl went off to play.

A few nights later one of the oldest men in the village came up to the boy as he sat by the fire. "What are those tassels on your arms, boy?"

"What do you see, Grandfather?

The old man thought for a moment. "They are the waves of the great waters." He paused, seemed to think again, then stared deeply at the boy's tassels, smiled and went on. "Yes, they are the waves of the great waters. And look! There! There are the great canoes my grandfather's grandfather crossed those great waters in, the same canoes which bade him safe passage to this place." The old man looked into the boy's eyes. "That's what I see."

"Thank you, Grandfather," said the even older boy. "Thank you so much for sharing with me what you see in these tassels on my arms. I did not know what they were and now I do. Thank you for telling me what you see."

The old man and the now-older boy hugged each other and the old man walked away, smiling as he remembered the great biadarkas which brought his people to this place where they lived.

And so it came, over time, that each person in the village told the boy what magic they saw in his tassels and he thanked them for the stories they told.

All, that is, except three old women. Each time they saw the boy they laughed. Finally one of the women asked, "What are those cords wrapped around your wrists?"

The boy shook his head. "I don't know, Grandmother. I always let people tell me what they are, that way I learn. What do you think they are?"

The old women huddled amongst themselves in whispers for a moment then laughed. "We thought they were strings to bind your sandals, but see you wear none. Probably just strings you found, are they not?"

The now grown boy saddened and counted this lesson as perhaps the greatest of all. He lifted his tassels and stared at them before he answered. "Why, yes, Grandmothers. If that is what you see, that's what they are."

The three old women cackled to themselves and walked away.

One day a great trouble came to the village. It came quickly and swiftly and no one was warned. Many in the village had already died when the little girl who had first spoken to the boy ran up to him and cried out, "Boy! Boy! You must do something quickly. Hurry! Our village is dying."

The old boy shook his head sadly, no. "But there's nothing I can do."

"Can you save us?"

Again the boy shook his head. "No. Each person has to save themself."

"How?" cried the little girl.

The old boy unwrapped the tassels from his wrists so they flowed like snakes upon the ground. "Tell me what you see, little one?"

"Snakes!" she screamed. "Beautiful, wonderful snakes!"

And so there were. Two huge glorious snakes coiling on the ground. They lifted their great heads up to face the little girl and slithery said, "Come, little daughter, get on our backs and ride us to safety."

And so she did and so she is safe. The terror engulfing the village reached her not.

Then came the old man. "Boy! Boy! How can I save myself?"

The old boy swayed his tassels before the old man's eyes. "What do you see, Grandfather?"

The old man calmed and smiled. "I see the waves of the great waters, and on them the canoes that first carried us to safety here."

And thus it was so. Suddenly the old boy and the old man were up to their waists in the sea with a great biadarka floating beside them. The old boy helped the old man and all in his family into their canoe. Suddenly a great wave came and the old man, his family, and their canoe sailed away. The old man turned and waved and then the very old boy was back in his village. The old man, all his people, the great biadarka that carried them, and the waters they sailed were gone.

Each person who came to the boy now came again. As each came the boy reminded them of the magic they saw in his tassels. Each person took their magic and went away to safety. There were great eagles and stars and waterfalls and buffalo, walking trees and talking waters, all flowing from the ancient boy's tassels to the people in the village.

All except the three old women. They came to him crying and screaming, "Tell us what magic you have for us, boy, that we might be safe as are the others."

The old boy remembered these three old women but there was nothing he could do.

"Surely there is some magic in those strands for us," they demanded.

The old boy shook his head and cried. "No, the only magic in my tassels is that which others put there. All the magic I gave others they already had. I merely reminded them of the magic within them. You saw nothing in my tassels, so there's nothing I can give you. There is no magic in you for me to remind you."

The boy grabbed his tassels and tied them around his hands. Suddenly his hands and tassels became great feathered wings which carried him away from the danger to where he was safe.

It's a Man's World

"Where are you going?"

Susan's face softened but she looked away.

All the women in the neighborhood were dressed in what we use to call "Easter Sunday" clothes; light dresses, bright, Spring colors of sky blues and yellows and whites, some with flower prints with big roses or tulips or daffodils or morning glories or black-eyed susans and all with long, lush green vines wrapping around them. All of them wearing wide-brimmed sun hats, many with scarves tying their hats around their chins. A few wore sunglasses. All had nice big purses, lots of different colors but most of them white, white cloth gloves covering their hands and all of them in either tasteful heels or flats. Nobody wore stilettos or CFMs of any kind.

And they gathered in front of my house.

It started with AnElla. I was walking the dog and she came out of her house in her Easter Sunday finest. I waved and she ignored me, walked back into her house and came back out with all her daughters, her granddaughters, her sisters, even her ailing mother-in-law. They were all standing nice and neat and trim and proper in front of her house.

A few minutes later all the other women in the neighborhood came out of their homes and stood in front of their houses. Mothers, daughters, grandmothers, aunts, sisters, they looked around, waved at each other, a few looked at the sky – not a cloud to be seen, by the way. Clear sky, bright sun. Clearest I'd seen in years, really - and one by one then two by two they moseyed over to my house.

Susan came out dressed like all the rest. Sunday is her day to sleep in. I didn't even know she had those kinds of clothes anymore.

A bus pulled up. An open air bus, a kind of parade or tourist bus with a roof but no windows. The paintjob matched the women's dresses; blues and yellows and whites and flowers everywhere. No city markings whatsoever.

Women gathered around the bus. Some got in. Susan stood in line with them.

"Where you going?"

"Don't worry. It's okay. You'll be fine."

You'll be fine?

"No, come on. Where you going?"

Tears welled up in her eyes. She looked away. "It's okay, Paul. I'll be back soon."

Now here's the thing about Susan: she can't lie. She never could. Not to me, anyway. Not to anybody who knows her, not to anybody she's ever known, and now she was lying to me and she knew it and she knew I knew it.

None of the other husbands were out of their houses yet. I don't think they knew. I wouldn't have known if I didn't have to take the dog for a walk first thing in the morning. I still had him on a leash and the women were petting him as they walked past. Some of them looked at me when they petted him and I had the feeling they were really petting me, or would have if they could, tolerant of a dumb animal that is loyal but can't understand.

I reached out for her. "What's going on, Princess? Tell me. We've never kept secrets from each other."

The other women grouped around her, not letting me touch her.

"Hey, what is this?"

One of the women, someone I hadn't noticed before, honestly someone I'd never seen in the neighborhood before, tall and slim and dark complexioned without being tanned, her face hidden by the brim of her hat, said, "Don't let him touch you. He'll understand if he touches you and we can't let him touch you, any of you."

I looked into the bus. No driver, no steering wheel, no driver's seat. With no branding on the side? Nobody spends money on a driverless bus without telling the world about it.

"Who's driving you?"

Susan said, "One of the others."

"What others?"

Two more tall, thin, dark complexioned women got in my way. I pushed one of them back, wanting to get to Susan. The woman fell, her hat coming loose and exposing her face.

She had cats' eyes and whiskers. And pointed ears.

"What the f...?"

Susan came to me, standing between the others and me, protecting me from them. "He's not like the rest," she pleaded. "He's not."

Cats'Eyes got up. She took her right glove off and slowly reached out to me, offering me her hand.

I took it. My mind caught fire, July 4th went off in my head. Sounds and colors and thoughts I didn't know existed.

The bus took off. Vertically. Just lifted off the ground and went up into the sky until not even a speck remained. No sound, no whoosh, no engines firing, no liftoff, no Houston-we-got-a-problem, no nothing. The trees didn't even move.

Guys came out of their houses, unshaven, some scratching t-shirt covered stomachs, some still in slippers and bathrobes, all holding empty coffee cups in one hand and some holding remotes in the other.

"Anybody seen Josie?" "Anybody seen Kate?" "Anybody seen Beka?" "Anybody seen..."

Cats'Eye's mindfire flickered in my head.

I understood.

Males existed, they simply weren't dominant. Nor did they dominate. And it was the first time I realized how similar those words are.

About Northern Lights Publishing

Northern Lights Publishing/Press is an association of five professionals (one graphic artist, one marketer, one editor/book designer, one copyeditor, one editor/educator/author) and a rotating group of ten published authors and poets all of whom are passionate readers. Financial backing is provided by a small group of investors led by Susan and Joseph Carrabis through the NextStage Evolution Corporation. Everyone receives remuneration and owns an equal share of the company with the exception of Susan and Joseph Carrabis.

We're developing our publishing/marketing model so we're not accepting submissions at present.

We'll open our doors to submissions (and announce it through various social networks) once we're sure we can break even and preferably turn a profit. Until then, wish us well.

It's an exciting journey and one we'd love to share, but only after we're sure we can successfully navigate the publishing seas.

About the Author

Joseph Carrabis told stories to anyone who would listen starting in childhood, wrote his first stories in gradeschool, and started getting paid for his writing in 1978. His work history includes periods as a long-haul trucker, apprentice butcher, apprentice coffee buyer/broker, lumberjack, Cold Regions researcher, mathematician, semanticist, semioticist, physicist, educator, Chief Data Scientist, Chief Research Scientist, and Chief Research Officer. He was an original member of the NYAS/UN's Scientists Without Borders program and held patents covering mathematics, anthropology, neuroscience, and linguistics. After patenting a technology he created in his basement and creating an international company, he retired from corporate life. Now he spends his time writing fiction based on his experiences. His work appears regularly in anthologies and his own novels. You can often find him playing with his dog, Boo, and snuggling with his wife, Susan. Learn more about him at https://joseph carrabis.com and his work at http://nlb.pub/amazon.

Follow Joseph on

BookBub http://nlb.pub/BookBub
Facebook http://nlb.pub/Facebook
Goodreads http://nlb.pub/Goodreads
Instagram http://nlb.pub/Instagram
Linkedin http://nlb.pub/LinkedIn
Pinterest http://nlb.pub/Pinterest
Twitter http://nlb.pub/Twitter

Did you enjoy That Th!nk You Do Volume 2: Romance & Relationships?

Please, write a review on
Amazon http://nlb.pub/TTYDv2
and
Goodreads http://nlb.pub/GTTYDv2
(and our thanks!)

You can find links to the blog posts mentioned in this book, as well as *That Th!nk You Do* trainings and contact info for Joseph to speak at your on- and off-line events at
http://nlb.pub/TTYD

Become a member of Joseph's blog -
http://nlb.pub/JoinJoseph

www.ingramcontent.com/pod-product-compliance
Lightning Source LLC
Chambersburg PA
CBHW070115030426
42335CB00016B/2162